KINGSNAKES
AND
MILK SNAKES

RONALD G. MARKEL

To my wife, Maria Teresa, and daughters, Samantha and Rebecca

Distributed in the UNITED STATES by T.F.H. Publications, Inc., One T.F.H. Plaza, Neptune City, NJ 07753; in CANADA to the Pet Trade by H & L Pet Supplies Inc., 27 Kingston Crescent, Kitchener, Ontario N2B 2T6; Rolf C. Hagen Ltd., 3225 Sartelon Street, Montreal 382 Quebec; in CANADA to the Book Trade by Macmillan of Canada (A Division of Canada Publishing Corporation), 164 Commander Boulevard, Agincourt, Ontario M1S 3C7; in ENGLAND by T.F.H. Publications Limited, Cliveden House/Priors Way/Bray, Maidenhead, Berkshire SL6 2HP, England; in AUSTRALIA AND THE SOUTH PACIFIC by T.F.H. (Australia) Pty. Ltd., Box 149, Brookvale 2100 N.S.W., Australia; in NEW ZEALAND by Ross Haines & Son, Ltd., 82 D Elizabeth Knox Place, Panmure, Auckland, New Zealand; in the PHILIPPINES by Bio-Research, 5 Lippay Street, San Lorenzo Village, Makati Rizal; in SOUTH AFRICA by Multipet Pty. Ltd., Box 235 New Germany, South Africa 3620. Published by T.F.H. Publications, Inc. Manufactured in the United States of America by T.F.H. Publications, Inc.

Contents

Acknowledgments

It is with gratitude that I wish to express my thanks to those individuals who contributed material and suggestions toward helping make this book as complete as possible. I would especially like to thank: Bob Applegate, Scott Ballard, John Breen, Dave Breidenbach, Glen Carlzen, Joseph T. Collins, Mike Dee, Ms. Patsy Eppinger, Dr. Richard Funk DVM, Prof. Huntsacker, Terry Lilley, Larry Manning, Sean McKeown, Jim Murphy, John C. Murphy, Mario Nevarez, John Ruiz, Vince Scheidt, Don Soderberg, Stu Tennyson, and Gary and Kerry Young. My apologies to those individuals I may have inadvertently forgotten to mention. Last but not least, many thanks to Jan Hayden for her help in editing, formatting, arranging, and typing, for without her persistence and patience this book could not have been finished.

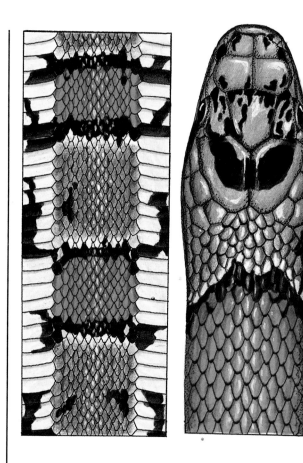

A Note on the Paintings

The color paintings of anterior and midbody views of each subspecies were done by John R. Quinn from the best available descriptions and illustrations, both published and unpublished, but they are still intended to be schematics, not portraits. Because of the great variation present in virtually all the *Lampropeltis* subspecies, it must be expected that individual specimens will differ to some degree from any painting or photograph. This is the first time that all valid taxa of *Lampropeltis* have been illustrated in color, especially the milk snakes.

Introduction

The increased growth in interest and general awareness of the outdoors and of the more attractive reptiles that inhabit these areas has inspired this book on the kingsnakes and milk snakes. Camping, hiking, backpacking, motor travel, and the now easy accessibility of many previously remote areas have led to a corresponding interest in reptiles encountered in the course of these pursuits.

The primary purpose of this book is identification of kingsnakes and milk snakes, a group of harmless snakes belonging to the strictly American genus *Lampropeltis*. Legislation for the protection of snakes often shows a strong consideration for economically important and esthetically valuable reptiles, especially those useful in controlling rodent populations. The expansion of human populations, destruction of natural habitats, and occasional over-collecting for economic and personal gratification, as well as the still persistent prejudice among uninformed people, have all combined to diminish the numbers of wild-living snakes. It is my hope that the material presented in this book will help bring about a better appreciation of at least one group of these colorful and harmless creatures.

Unlike most other groups of snakes, kingsnakes are currently being bred in fair numbers by many dedicated hobbyists. In some subspecies one could make a case that there may be as many or more individuals currently in captivity than have ever been collected in the wild. I have attempted to assemble a guide that will be helpful both to hobbyists and to herpetologists with specific interests in the natural history of kingsnakes and milk snakes. Technical studies on *Lampropeltis* are numerous, and there is an ever-increasing number of papers on their taxonomy, distribution, and natural history. In what follows I have attempted to make some of this literature available to the interested reader, while emphasizing identification of all the currently valid forms of the genus. A few problematical forms have also been included because, even though they are not at the moment considered

valid subspecies, they are being kept and bred by hobbyists as pure forms and the hobbyist literature often talks about these forms. Since these problematical forms are often from very restricted ranges and may be rare in nature, their preservation in captivity may be their only chance at survival.

Introducing kingsnakes

The kingsnakes and milk snakes comprise the genus *Lampropeltis*, a strictly American genus that ranges from southern Ontario and southwestern Quebec west to southern Washington (south of the 48th parallel) and south to northwestern South America in Colombia, Ecuador, and the Cordillera de la Costa of Venezuela (Blaney, 1973). They are powerful constrictors that feed on a variety of vertebrates and, to a lesser extent, invertebrates. They inhabit a wide variety of habitats, from arid regions to rain forest and marshland, at elevations from below sea level to at least 8500 feet (2550 meters) in the Rocky Mountains and 10,000 feet (3000 meters) in the Andes Mountains of South America.

Lampropeltis (the name is derived from the Greek *lampros* or shiny, plus *pelta* or shield) is a group of rather generalized colubrid snakes characterized by smooth scales each with two apical pits. The dorsal scales are arranged in 17 to 27 rows. The ventrals are not especially angular and usually have at least some dark pigment. The anal plate is entire and the subcaudals are divided. Kingsnakes and milk snakes are small to moderately large snakes with moderately short tails. The maxillary teeth number 12 to 20, the dentary teeth 12 to 18, the palatine teeth 8 to 14, and the pterygoid teeth 12 to 23. Except for two enlarged posterior maxillary teeth in some species, the teeth are not exceptional. The hemipenis is asymmetrically bilobed, either shallowly or distinctly.

Currently there are eight living species of kingsnakes and milk snakes recognized as valid by authorities. Two other species (*L. intermedius*

Brattstrom, 1955, from Michoacan, Mexico, and Cochise County, Arizona, in the Upper Pliocene; and *L. similis* Holman, 1964, from the Mio-Pliocene of Nebraska, both related to the *L. triangulum* group) are known only as fossils and do not concern us. The species treated as valid in this book are: *L. alterna* (no subspecies); *L. calligaster* (two or possibly three subspecies); *L. getulus* (seven subspecies plus four problematical forms); *L. mexicana* (no subspecies but two problematical forms); *L. pyromelana* (four subspecies); *L. ruthveni* (a poorly known and rather problematical species); *L. triangulum* (25 subspecies); and *L. zonata* (seven subspecies). These species are usually placed in two groups, the *getulus* group (*calligaster, getulus*) without enlarged posterior maxillary teeth, and the *triangulum* group (all other species) with enlarged posterior maxillary teeth. *L. alterna* and *mexicana* are often considered to be intermediate between these two groups, with relationships to both *L. calligaster* and *L. triangulum* noted by various workers.

At the present time there is no one work that surveys all the species and subspecies of kingsnakes, although there are many separate studies of the various species and groups of subspecies. The last full revision of the genus was by Blanchard in 1921. It is not the purpose here to present the same material contained in these works, but to summarize and condense the important characteristics for all the taxa of the genus and provide information on their natural history and care in captivity. (Many kinds of kingsnakes and milk snakes are relatively common and are frequently displayed in zoos, as well as maintained in private collections.) Range maps are based on the relevant revisions and/or Conant (1975), Stebbins (1966), and Wright and Wright (1957). Common names are given for all taxa, including subspecies, because they are often used by hobbyists. Common names for United States taxa follow Collins, et al. (1978) and Frank Slaven's *Inventory of Reptiles and Amphibians in Captivity (1982-1984)*.

Before collecting or purchasing a kingsnake it is wise to check with your local wildlife or fish and game agency to determine if there are restrictions on what can be taken or even kept. In some states kingsnakes are rigidly protected, and in many states permits are needed before a snake can even be purchased. Local and national laws are often contradictory and are always changing, but you should at least make an effort to determine your local situation—penalities are often harsh. Allen (1986) is a good starting point for reviewing relevant laws.

With the increase in captive-breeding success over the last decade, kingsnakes and milk snakes now are probably the most commonly available pet snakes. Captive-bred kings are of much higher quality, have fewer legal restrictions on their sale, and usually have better temperaments than wild-caught specimens. Photo of *Lampropeltis mexicana "greeri"* by Alex Kerstitch.

Milk snakes such as this gorgeous specimen of *L. triangulum annulata* are commonly known as tricolors or tricolored kings because of the red-black-yellow banding characteristic of their patterns. Tricolors tend to be harder to feed and maintain than non-tricolors, but their great beauty makes them more desirable. Photo by B. Kahl.

Kingsnakes have gained a reputation as eaters of venomous snakes, including such species as the water moccasin, *Agkistrodon piscivorus conanti*, shown here. Fortunately, snakes are not a necessary part of the *Lampropeltis* diet. Photo by S. Kochetov.

Although kingsnakes show few or no ill effects from the bites of North American pit vipers such as this *Crotalus viridis*, their immunity to the venom of foreign venomous species, especially cobras and relatives, is variable. Photo by S. Kochetov.

This dark phase *L. alterna* is typical of a captive-bred kingsnake. Because of captive-breeding several species and subspecies of kings are now available in many color phases (including albinos) that are seldom seen in nature. Photo by R. W. Applegate.

Physiognomy of a typical *Lampropeltis*. The head shape and scalation are not too different from that of typical colubrids. Photo by R. G. Markel of *L. g. californiae*.

Head scales of a typical unspecialized colubrid snake.

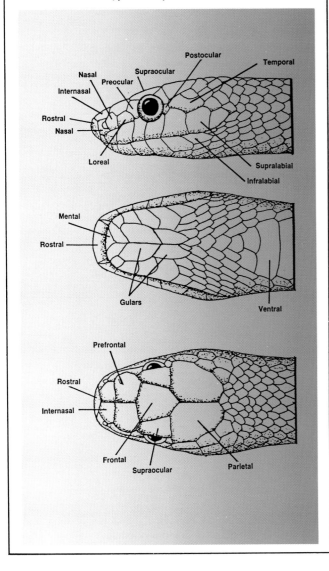

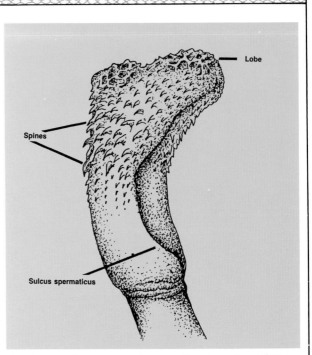

Hemipene of *L. getulus* showing the typical condition of relatively large spines and one well-developed lobe.

Female (left) and male (right) tail shapes in *Lampropeltis*.

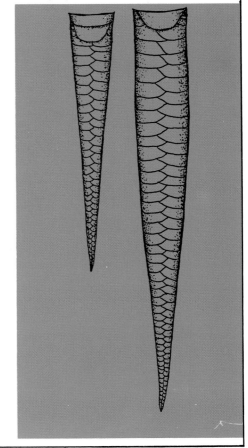

Identification of tricolor kings lacking locality data usually is difficult and may even be impossible at the subspecific level. The most important features to note are the head pattern, including color of snout, the number of red and yellow (or white) rings, whether the black pigment expands into the red or appears as stippling within the red and yellow rings, and the ventral pattern. Counts of rings and of ventral and subcaudal scales usually are the most important identifying characters in the technical literature but are highly variable and must be used with caution if applied to only one or two specimens. Photo of *L. pyromelana* probably *infralabialis* by Alex Kerstitch.

A cleared and stained snake shows the numerous flexibly articulated vertebrae and ribs typical of all snakes. Note that the lower jaws are not strongly attached to the skull, part of the feeding adaptation that makes snakes such versatile predators. Photo by Guido Dingerkus.

No, you do not have to worry about supplying venomous snakes (such as this timber rattler, *Crotalus horridus*) to your kingsnake. Although kings are snake-eaters (ophiophages) in nature, your pet will never have to eat a snake if you don't want it to. In fact, today most keepers would question the ethics of feeding one snake to another under almost any circumstances. Since they are ophiophagous, however, kingsnakes should never be caged with smaller kingsnakes—even of the same species—without constant supervision.

Small, abundant lizards such as young *Sceloporus undulatus* can be collected (sparingly) or bred as food for tricolor kings, many of which may prefer an occasional lizard to a constant mouse diet. Photo by Guido Dingerkus.

Kingsnakes in captivity

The varied patterns and rich colors of the kingsnakes, plus their adaptability to captivity, make them by far the most displayed group of harmless snakes. With some 50 taxa known that range from Canada to Ecuador and vary in length from 6 feet (1.8 meters) to just 20 inches (50 cm), there is something here to please any fancier.

Feeding

An interesting point about the kingsnakes is their feeding habits. Because all kingsnakes are both ophiophagous (basically, feeding on almost any snake) and generalized carnivores, they are one of the easiest types of snakes to maintain in captivity. They can consume warm-blooded prey such as rodents and birds in addition to cold-blooded frogs, lizards, and snakes. One drawback of this is that they are also highly cannibalistic and can not be housed more than one snake per cage. They are among the few snakes immune to the venom of various venomous snakes, especially the pit vipers.

Many factors contribute to the development of a baby snake's feeding habits. Water must be available at all times. Both cage size and environment are important. The cage should be clean, dry, 80-90°F (preferably with subfloor heat), and have a secure place for the snake to hide in both the warm and cool zones of the cage. This relatively high temperature range helps to prevent regurgitation and gastrointestinal problems. The substrate can be silica sand, newspaper, or pine shavings. Do not use cedar shavings, and avoid any treated substances such as cat litter.

All food items offered must be of easily swallowed size and should not cause large "lumps" of food in the snake's intestines. The food item can be left in the cage for several hours, but the cage should be undisturbed during that time, preferably with no one in the same room.

Some snakes feed nocturnally, so you may have to try the following techniques for getting a snake to feed both at night and during the day.

Although there is no doubt that mice make the most satisfactory long-term diet for most kingsnakes, not all specimens adjust well to such a diet. Because many kingsnakes, especially young of all species and all ages of milk snakes, prefer a diet based on cold-blooded foods, some hobbyists like to supply lizards at regular intervals. Where small lizards are abundant and readily collected without environmental impact, species of *Uta* (below) and *Sceloporus* may be taken during season and either maintained in a colony or frozen for later feeding. Photo by F. J. Dodd, Jr.

Hatchling *Sceloporus* are readily accepted by many small kingsnakes. Photo by Ken Lucas, Steinhart Aquarium.

Best feeding results occur after shedding is completed, as ecdysis often causes a loss of appetite. It is best to not attempt to feed an "opaque" or "dead-eyed" snake.

Enticing a snake with dead food by means of forceps is helpful. The preferred method is to feed the meal to the snake head-first, regardless whether it is a mouse, lizard, or chick. The snake may strike out of retaliation and seize the prey. Rubbing the snake's sensitive points (labial or lip area, neck, tail) with the food item may encourage feeding. If a snake refuses to feed, it may be sexually active, the excitement causing it to lose interest in feeding. Time alone may bring a snake to hunger.

The following are suggestions that may be used in the event that a snake (especially a baby) is refusing food or in an attempt to adapt it from more natural foods to pinkies. However, avoid force-feeding whenever possible as it may cause injury or dependency.

1) Most babies will feed on live newborn mice (pinkies). Place a live pinkie in the opening of the snake's favorite hiding place. If uneaten in a few hours, replace it with a dead pinkie.

2) Wash a pinkie in soap and water and rinse well. Dry it and place it in the opening of the hide. Washing removes some of the domestic mouse scent. Try a living, then a dead pinkie.

3) Get a feeder lizard (*Uta* or *Sceloporus*) and rub it all over a washed and dried pinkie. Try cutting off a small piece of the lizard's tail and rubbing some of the blood on the face of the pinkie. Put a piece of the tail in the pinkie's mouth.

4) Kill a pinkie and cut open the top of the

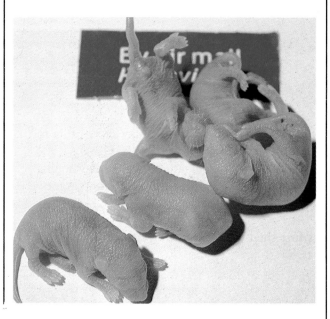

Above: Mice only a few hours to a few days old are known as "pinkies" until fur develops. Photo by M. Gilroy.

Left: An occasional pet shop lizard, such as an *Anolis carolinensis*, may be offered to larger kingsnakes for variety. Photo by Isabelle Francais.

head. Mush the brains and place the pinkie in the hiding place. This grizzly technique works surprisingly often, but use it as a last resort.

5) If the snake still hasn't fed, offer it any natural food item you think it might accept, just to get a meal into it. Offer the item (a small lizard, treefrog, baby wild mouse, etc.) by hand at first. If the snake will accept the food from your hand, it will be easy to offer two food items at the same time, one the accepted food and the other a pinkie. Cause the snake to miss its target during its lunge and take the pinkie next to it. Always leave a pinkie in the cage after the snake has accepted a different food item. Often the snake will follow the first meal with a pinkie.

Usually a snake will have fed before you reach this point. Once it has eaten, get it to accept plain pinkies. However, if it has not yet eaten, mist the cage heavily with a water spray to raise the humidity. Then repeat the above steps. Don't keep the snake in a wet, warm cage for more than a few days. Sometimes placing in the cage a moss-filled opaque plastic container with a small entrance hole cut in it serves to give the snake a better hiding place and encourages a feeding response when a pinkie is dropped inside with the snake. Some baby snakes react badly to constant contact with damp moss, being unable to shed, having a premature shed, or developing sticky skin or skin blisters. It is very important to keep an eye on them.

If your snake hasn't eaten within four weeks of its first shed (usually five to twelve days after hatching), you may have to force-feed. Gently use the nose of a dead pinkie or other small dull object to open the snake's mouth. When the pinkie's head is inside the snake's mouth, gently apply pressure to the outside of the upper and lower jaws of the snake with your fingers and gently pull out on the pinkie. This will stick the pinkie on the snake's teeth, making it more difficult to regurgitate. Wait until the snake isn't struggling and gently put it down in the cage. Don't move! You may have to repeat this several times. Usually the snake will give up and swallow the pinkie. If this fails, start the pinkie the same way, then gently shove it down the snake's throat using a very dull object. Gently massage the pinkie down to a quarter or third of the snake's length.

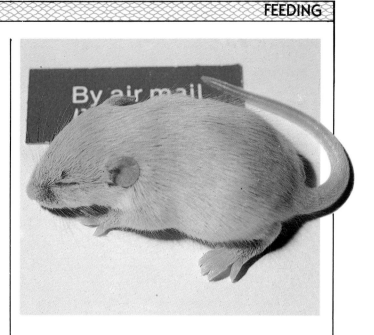

By the time a young mouse has a good coat of hair, it is too large for most tricolor kings and small individuals of other species. Kingsnakes can be trained to take frozen and thawed pinkies or young furred mice (fuzzies), so most keepers would not let their mice reach the age shown here. Photos by M. Gilroy.

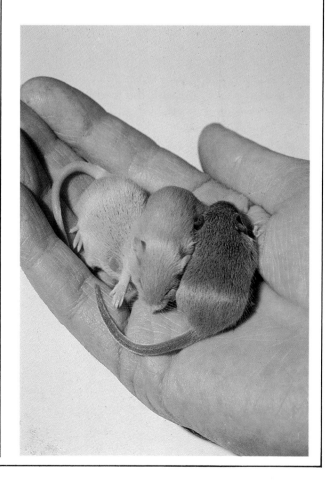

Above: Mice and kingsnakes go together. If you have the room and can stand the smell, consider breeding your own mice if you plan on large-scale captive-breeding. **Right**: *L. pyromelana* taking a small mouse. Photos by Dr. H. R. Axelrod (top) and B. E. Baur.

If feeding is a continuing problem, there are "pinkie pumps" available that literally liquefy a pinkie so it can be pumped down the snake's throat. These are expensive, but they are useful when force-feeding baby snakes "assembly-line style," keeping them alive and growing until they will accept pinkies on their own.

Some baby snakes, particularly those hatched late in the season, will not accept pinkies regularly until the following spring. In the winter snakes enter semihibernation and the need for food is reduced. The diet and regularity of feeding may vary from snake to snake during this period. If too much moisture should develop in your cage and the problem is not rectified, your snake may acquire a respiratory or skin infection.

The average kingsnake will shed its skin within two weeks of coming out of hibernation, especially if heavily fed. Photo *L. getulus getulus* by Ken Lucas, Steinhart Aquarium.

Hibernation and breeding

Like most snakes, kingsnakes mate during the spring of the year and are oviparous. Eggs are laid in the spring, summer, and fall months. However, controlled conditions in captivity may produce eggs at other times of the year.

The general health of a reptile is the most important factor in breeding. Breeding is a strain on their health. If they are not in prime

L. t. sinaloae in a very serviceable cage setup. Photo by J. Gee.

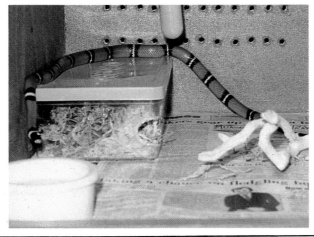

condition, they could develop serious problems. Snakes are not like mammals that come into sexual season at regular intervals. They produce sex cells when they have the right environmental conditions and enough body weight to afford the stress of reproduction.

Breeding-potential kingsnakes, being temperate climate species, should be kept at 78-82°F day and night, with a long light cycle of up to 16 hours per day. Providing food on a constant basis is very important for the snake. It should receive a medium meal every four to six days except when shedding. The snakes should be kept in a low-stress environment away from other animals and people. This allows the snakes to become better acclimated and more sensitive to environmental changes. Most snakes breed better when the sexes are separated during the non-breeding season.

Hibernation is a very important step in breeding kingsnakes. The method discussed here has been used successfully in central California but may vary due to geographic area, altitude, and background climate.

A kingsnake chosen for breeding next season is

A mating pair of *L. t. gentilis*, the male with a firm grasp on the female's head. Photo by L. Trutnau.

hibernated from December through February at temperatures from 55-62°F with no lighting. All through November the snake is kept warmer than normal with a long light cycle. The snake is not fed during this period so the stomach will be empty when put into hibernation. Snake digestive enzymes work at certain temperatures, and food will rot in the digestive tract at cold temperatures and may kill the snake. Each kingsnake is housed individually in a small

The intertwined bodies and cloacas in full contact indicate that these *L. t. sinaloae* are mating. Photo by L. Trutnau.

plastic container that is misted slightly and placed in a cool, dark garage. For the next three months the undisturbed snake lies calm, living off its excess body fat. Hibernation is undoubtedly a stress on even a healthy snake, but if the snake is not healthy it may die during hibernation.

Snakes need a dormant period for the brain to trigger hormonal production that then causes sex cells to be produced. Once these cells are produced, the female will produce sex hormones that act something like a perfume to attract males. Once a male comes into contact with a producing female, breeding almost always takes place. This whole process is stimulated by the hibernation or dormant period. Without a hibernation period, most snakes will not produce sex cells, but they may still breed. Usually these breedings go to waste and no eggs are produced.

After the snakes have hibernated, they are put back into their normal environment. They quickly become active and start feeding. After several feedings, usually after about two weeks, they will shed their skin. During this period it is important to have water available for drinking because the females are starting egg production. After this first shed, breeding usually begins. The female enlarges in girth and becomes very active. Some snakes will breed two or three weeks after hibernation, while others may go six to eight weeks. Many small meals should be

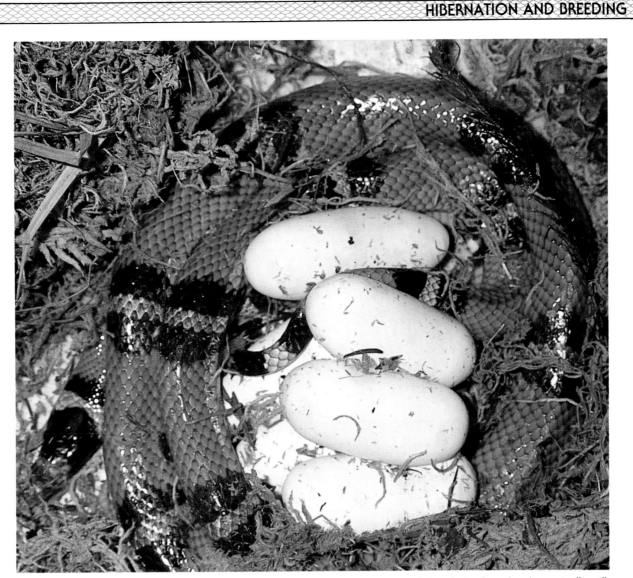

If the eggs are left with the female, she typically will coil about them, providing some extra control of humidity and perhaps also providing them some protection from small predators. The elongate shape of the eggs of this *L. t. sinaloae* is fairly typical of kingsnakes. Photo by L. Trutnau.

given to the females during this period. If they do not get enough food, they may resorb their developing eggs. Once the females become active and constantly cruise their cages, they are placed into the male's cage, one at a time. If the female is producing eggs, copulation usually occurs in several minutes to several hours. If the male shows no interest in the female, she probably is not producing eggs yet. Separate the snakes and resume feeding of the female. Breed each female several times over a two-month period to ensure high fertility.

Hatchling kingsnakes literally cut their way out of the egg with an egg tooth that is lost within hours of hatching. Because there is still yolk in the gut, hatchlings usually do not feed for the first ten days or so, at which time they have their first shed and will need their first meal. The patterns of the hatchling *L. alterna* (above) and *L. t. sinaloae* (below) are much as in the adults, although the tones of the colors may differ. Photo above by R. G. Markel, that below by L. Trutnau.

Once the females have bred, they should be separated into their own cages. To ensure egg development and proper growth of the embryos, give the females plenty of food and water. Some snakes will not eat when they are gravid (pregnant), and little can be done about it. The snake will drink plenty of water and use up its own body fat for energy. Care should be taken not to handle a gravid snake, because too much handling can lead to bad eggs or dead babies.

Most kingsnakes and milk snakes can be expected to shed about four weeks after their first breeding. Usually the females lay their eggs from one to three weeks after this shed. It is very important to put a nest box in with the gravid female.

A successful method of trying to hatch a brood of eggs is to use vermiculite. Alternative methods using moss and sand have also proved successful. Basically, you want the eggs to be kept moist, but not wet. Humidity is an important factor. The container is also determined by individual preference. You can use clear plastic shoe boxes, glass aquariums, gallon jars, or styrofoam boxes. Moisten a 3-inch layer of vermiculite and place the eggs in it as they were laid, half buried in the vermiculite. Do not separate any eggs that are stuck together and do not rotate, disturb, or alter the position of the eggs. Keep the container covered with a sheet of glass or plastic that will help maintain proper humidity. Most eggs can be hatched at temperatures from 60 to 90°F. The warmer the

Instead of leaving the eggs with the female, most keepers remove the eggs for incubation on a bed of vermiculite or a similar substance. This makes it easier to maintain the proper humidity and to check the development of the eggs. In large-scale breeding operations it also makes it easier to "file" clutches of eggs to keep track of the bloodlines of the parents. Photo of *L. g. getulus* hatchlings by J. Gee.

temperature, the quicker the eggs will hatch.

If the female does not have a moist, quiet place to lay her eggs, she will constantly cruise the cage looking for one. I have seen snakes get egg-bound and die because they could not find a suitable place to lay their eggs. Once the snake has found a nest site, she will coil up and lie there calmly. Her eggs are laid one at a time, taking as much as 24 hours for an entire clutch to be produced.

If the eggs are fertile, a nice white color, and growing in size, they should hatch in two to three months. If the eggs are infertile, they usually will rot in two to three weeks.

Newborn kingsnakes are from 6 to 10 inches (15-25 cm) long. Baby snakes shed their first skin about ten days after hatching and then feed for the first time. Several feedings per month of pinkies or lizards should be sufficient for the healthy growth of the young, but of course each snake will vary somewhat. Young kingsnakes should be kept separately just as adults.

Remember to give the female lots of food and water after she has produced the eggs. This will bring her body weight back up so she can be hibernated again for next year's breeding.

If a young snake should do poorly in captivity, it is best to try to release it in its area of origin (at least the origin of the parents). Most kingsnakes can be replaced fairly easily, so there is little sense in keeping a non-feeding snake so long that it starves. A pair of exhibition snakes and a back-up are sufficient for a collection of a species or subspecies. Many areas now have laws concerning collecting and keeping snakes because they are becoming endangered through loss of habitat and over-collecting. Please try to be considerate of these harmless, gentle creatures.

Albinism

Albinism can occur in cold-blooded as well as warm-blooded animals. There are, in fact, a variety of types of albinism, but the type we are discussing in relation to kingsnakes is the one that produces a basically white and opaque-looking specimen and often shows pink and yellow in the remnants of pattern. This is usually due to a hereditary failure to produce melanin. Melanin is the pigment that gives dark coloration to the skin. One normal gene (the dominant gene) controls the production of all the enzyme necessary to produce melanin. An abnormal gene (the recessive gene) producing albinism is not expressed phenotypically (visible in the external appearance of an animal) when present in combination with a dominant gene. (This abnormal recessive gene technically results in a lack of the amino acid tyrosinase, from which melanin is synthesized.) The dominant, melanin-producing gene and the recessive, non-melanin-producing gene are at the same place on the chromosome and are called alleles. When both alleles are abnormal (recessive), no enzyme

is produced and thus no melanin is deposited in the skin, resulting in an albino. In addition to the white appearance of the skin, the eyes of an albino are pink to red because blood shows through the capillaries of the eyes. Vision may be impaired in an albino because without the light-absorbing melanin, light is reflected about the interior of the eye instead of reaching the vision cells.

The breeding of albino kingsnakes is now well-established, and albinos of several species and subspecies are commercially available. The most popular albinos are probably those of *L. g. californiae*, with both striped (top) and ringed (left) color phases being bred. Good albino kingsnakes are famous for their brilliant yellow on pinkish patterns. Photo at top by Guido Dingerkus, that at left by Alex Kerstitch.

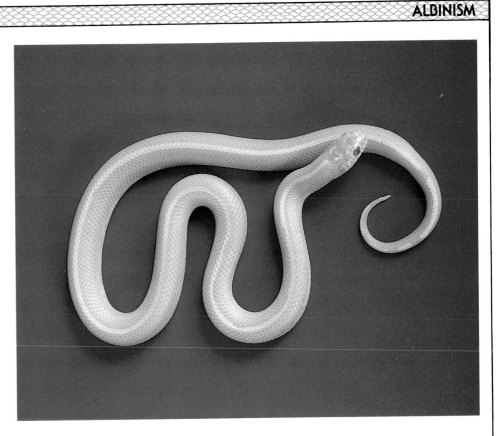

Albinos often are not as hardy as fully colored specimens and sometimes do not have the best temperaments. This specimen, for instance, still tries to bite its keeper and has never fully tamed. Photo of *L. g. californiae* by Ray Hunziker.

The genetics of albinism in kingsnakes usually is a simple dominant-recessive problem, so the results of breeding snakes of known bloodlines can be predicted to some extent. There apparently are several types of genetic patterns that can produce albinism, however, so occasionally breeding experiments do not come to expectations. Photo of *L. g. californiae* by Guido Dingerkus.

L. g. holbrooki also is produced as an albino, but the pattern is not as striking as in *californiae* albinos. Photo by G. Carlzen.

When the genes at one particular position on a chromosome are alike and control the same function in the same way, they are said to be homozygous; if the genes are different at the same position or locus, they are said to be heterozygous. Phenotype is the term used to refer to the visible characteristic expressed as a result of the action of the genes; genotype is the genetic condition that is not visible externally. Normal pigmentation occurs with genotypically either homozygous dominant genes or heterozygous genes. Albinism occurs only in situations where the genes are homozygous recessive. Symbols are used for genes when diagraming genetic crosses. Lower case letters are used for recessive genes, capital letters for dominant genes. Using Punnett squares, a type of checkerboard that you probably used in biology classes, we can represent the various genetic combinations possible during a cross. In our examples, A is dominant and means phenotypically normal color, while a is recessive and leads to albinism. Animals that are AA or Aa have normal coloration, while only those that are aa are albinos.

Albino kingsnakes are currently very popular and are bred in fairly large numbers. Genetically different parents when bred together can produce litters that are normal, normal but carrying an unexpressed gene for albinism, or albinos. Take for example a breeding involving parents that are both heterozygous, Aa. Our Punnett square shows the theoretical results of such a cross to yield offspring in the proportions:

¼ albino, homozygous recessive, aa
½ normal, carrying albinism, heterozygous, Aa
¼ normal, not carrying albinism, homozygous, AA.

For this type of simple albinism, the following common breeding combinations are possible:

Albino (aa) x Albino (aa): All albino, aa
Albino (aa) x Normal (AA): All normal, heterozygous, Aa
Heterozygous normal (Aa) x Heterozygous normal (Aa): 50% normal heterozygous (Aa), 25% normal homozygous (AA), 25% albino (aa)
Heterozygous normal (Aa) x Albino (aa): 50% heterozygous normal (Aa), 50% albino (aa)

Occasionally snakes of different strains present an unusual situation. Because the alleles are at different loci on the chromosomes, breeding an albino of one strain with an albino of another strain will result in normal young, not albinos. The young are all heterozygous for the two strains, however, and when crossed among themselves yield the following results:

This albino hatchling *holbrooki* has a vivid pattern, but as it grows older the contrast probably will decrease. Photo by R. G. Markel.

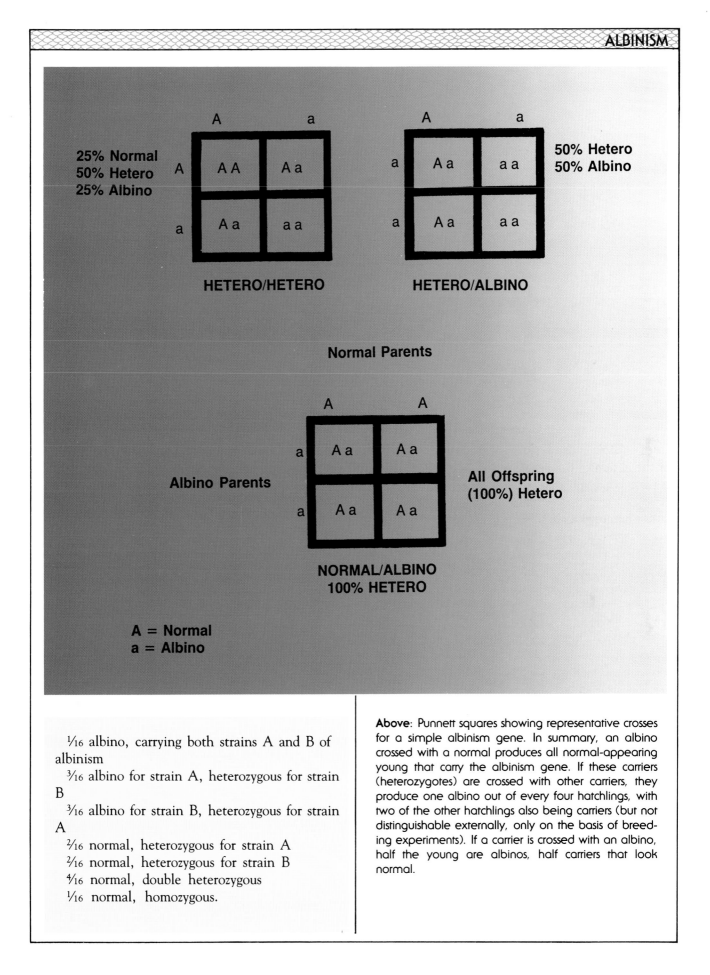

25% Normal
50% Hetero
25% Albino

HETERO/HETERO

50% Hetero
50% Albino

HETERO/ALBINO

Normal Parents

Albino Parents

All Offspring
(100%) Hetero

NORMAL/ALBINO
100% HETERO

A = Normal
a = Albino

$\frac{1}{16}$ albino, carrying both strains A and B of albinism

$\frac{3}{16}$ albino for strain A, heterozygous for strain B

$\frac{3}{16}$ albino for strain B, heterozygous for strain A

$\frac{2}{16}$ normal, heterozygous for strain A

$\frac{2}{16}$ normal, heterozygous for strain B

$\frac{4}{16}$ normal, double heterozygous

$\frac{1}{16}$ normal, homozygous.

Above: Punnett squares showing representative crosses for a simple albinism gene. In summary, an albino crossed with a normal produces all normal-appearing young that carry the albinism gene. If these carriers (heterozygotes) are crossed with other carriers, they produce one albino out of every four hatchlings, with two of the other hatchlings also being carriers (but not distinguishable externally, only on the basis of breeding experiments). If a carrier is crossed with an albino, half the young are albinos, half carriers that look normal.

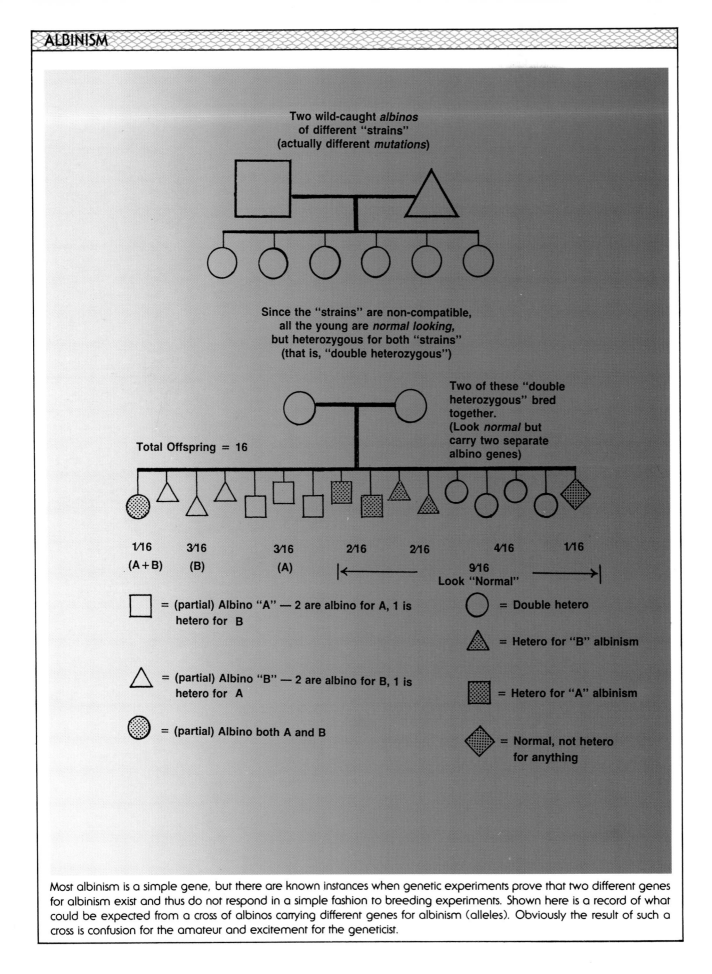

Two wild-caught *albinos*
of different "strains"
(actually different *mutations*)

Since the "strains" are non-compatible,
all the young are *normal looking*,
but heterozygous for both "strains"
(that is, "double heterozygous")

Two of these "double heterozygous" bred together.
(Look *normal* but carry two separate albino genes)

Total Offspring = 16

1/16
(A+B)

3/16
(B)

3/16
(A)

2/16

2/16

4/16

1/16

9/16
Look "Normal"

☐ = (partial) Albino "A" — 2 are albino for A, 1 is hetero for B

△ = (partial) Albino "B" — 2 are albino for B, 1 is hetero for A

⬤ = (partial) Albino both A and B

◯ = Double hetero

△ = Hetero for "B" albinism

▨ = Hetero for "A" albinism

◆ = Normal, not hetero for anything

Most albinism is a simple gene, but there are known instances when genetic experiments prove that two different genes for albinism exist and thus do not respond in a simple fashion to breeding experiments. Shown here is a record of what could be expected from a cross of albinos carrying different genes for albinism (alleles). Obviously the result of such a cross is confusion for the amateur and excitement for the geneticist.

Albinism is not the only pattern abnormality that occurs in kingsnakes. Melanism, an increase of the dark pigment over all or part of the body, also is fairly common, as in this *L. t. sinaloae* variant. If melanism develops heavily enough to obscure the pattern, the specimen may become unidentifiable. Melanism is normal in a few taxa, such as *L. t. gaigeae* and *L. c. rhombomaculata*. Photo by B. Kahl.

Another pattern variation, especially common in milk snakes, is the replacement of yellow or white with red pigments. In *L. t. hondurensis* this results in a striking phase called the "tangerine" by hobbyists. Such a specimen may be almost uniformly deep orange-red with even the black bands reduced. Such extreme specimens are seldom found, however, most specimens having just a partial replacement of yellow with red as in the specimen above. Photo by J. Gee.

Mimicry and Similar Species

The milk snakes and other tricolored kings have gained a reputation as mimics of coral snakes, both
groups commonly having red,
black, and yellow bands, but the
entire question of mimicry is a complex one that is not fully under-
stood. Here we will take a casual
look at the presence of "mimic"
patterns in a few other snakes and
some variations on the theme.

Above and below: *Rhinocheilus lec-
ontei*, the Long-nosed Snake, is often
considered the closest relative of the
kingsnakes. In typical patterns as
shown here, black saddles alternate
with irregular reddish blotches. Photos
by B. Kahl.

However, in some populations of
Long-nosed Snake (variably recognized as subspecies or simply color
phases) the black and red saddles become much more distinct and the yellowish to tan background color as-
sumes a ringed pattern. This "mimic"
pattern almost certainly has no func-
tional value in protecting the snake
from predators through a resemblance
to coral snakes. Photo above by J. K.
Langhammer.

Although at first glance this appears to be an example of mimicry, it is just a coincidence of matching an aberrant pattern with an unrelated snake. The snake above is a freak of *L. t. sinaloae* in which the black and yellow pigments are virtually undeveloped dorsally and are present only as remnants on the sides. The head pattern is fully developed. The snake below is *Pseudoboa neuwiedii*, an unrelated taxon found from Colombia to the Amazon, generally outside the range of the kingsnakes and certainly outside the range of *L. t. sinaloae*. Photo above by Alex Kerstitch, that below by R. S. Simmons.

There is no doubt that many *Lampropeltis* bear more than a passing resemblance to coral snakes, *Micrurus*. Many coral snakes are even sympatric (found in the same geographical area) and syntopic (found in the same habitat, even under the same log) with milk snakes that have superficially similar patterns. Note that in most coral snakes, including the southeastern United States *Micrurus fulvius*, above, red bands touch yellow bands, while in milk snakes the red bands touch black bands. Photo above by Ken Lucas, Steinhart Aquarium, that below of *Micrurus corallinus* by M. Freiberg.

The Arizona Coral Snake (*Micruroides euryxanthus*) in found in the range of both *L. triangulum* and *L. pyromelana* but does not bear a striking resemblance to any sympatric subspecies of either species. Photo by J. K. Langhammer.

In the coral snake *Micrurus frontalis* the red bands are bordered by black and the black and yellow bands occur in triads, much as in *L. zonata*. However, *L. zonata* is not sympatric with any coral snake, so it obviously cannot be a mimic. Photo by M. Freiberg.

One excellent example of what probably really is mimicry is provided by certain pattern types of *L. alterna* (above) and the rock rattler, *Crotalus lepidus*. These two species are unrelated but are sympatric and possibly syntopic, and there is no denying the similarity of the patterns and the advantages conferred to *L. alterna* by the resemblance. However, only a few individuals of *L. alterna* have a pattern resembling that of the rattlesnake at all closely. Photo above by S. Tennyson, that below by S. Kochetov.

The Mexican and Central American *Pliocercus elapoides* is another snake widely held to be a coral snake mimic, and certainly individuals such as this one do look like coral snakes in most details of the pattern. Again, however, the species (and its relatives) are highly variable and only some individuals and populations bear much similarity to sympatric coral snakes. Photo by L. Porras.

Ringed patterns often occur in snakes that no one would seriously call mimics, such as the rare burrower *Sonora (Procinura) aemula* from northwestern Mexico. No two individuals of this species are alike in color pattern, being with or without rings and head patterns. A black and white head pattern like this is found in many small Neotropical burrowing snakes. Photo by Ken Lucas, Steinhart Aquarium.

Extremes in development of the ringed pattern. In the burrowing, desert-dwelling *Chionactis occipitalis*, the Western Shovel-nosed Snake, the rings are actually distinct saddles on a yellowish straw background (above). *Rhinobotryum bovalli* from Central America (below) has a body pattern that almost exactly matches that of several milk snakes, yet the head pattern is unlike anything seen in *Lampropeltis*. Photo above by R. Holland, that below by B. Kahl.

The South and Central American species of *Erythrolamprus* are very similar to several milk snakes in shape and pattern and could easily be confused with them. They are considered by most authorities to be mimics of sympatric coral snakes and are close enough in pattern and even behavior (including displaying the underside of the tail as do coral snakes) to make the observer believe he actually is seeing a coral snake. Top left photo of *E. aesculapii* by S. Kochetov; top right photo of *E. mimus* by J. T. Kellnhauser; photo below of *E. aesculapii* by A. I. Grasso.

At least two other genera of South American snakes, these from south of the Amazon, have ringed patterns and are purported to be coral snake mimics. Above is *Oxyrhopus trigeminus*, which has interesting triads shared with several coral snakes. Below is *Lystrophis semicinctus*, which has a more typical ringed pattern. Photos by M. Freiberg.

The gorgeous Sinaloan Milk Snake,
Lampropeltis triangulum sinaloae.
Photo by B. Kahl.

Recognition of the kingsnakes

The following discussions of the species and subspecies of kingsnakes and milk snakes attempt to cover all the taxa in uniform fashion, with emphasis on the color patterns, the most obvious characters of most kingsnakes. Meristics have been taken from relevant technical sources and usually represent the range of variation, not just the most commonly seen variation. Thus if the number of ventrals of a subspecies are given as 200-225, this represents the range found by a researcher making counts on, for instance, 100 specimens. The actual counts found in the great majority of specimens might all be encompassed by 210-215. This should be remembered whenever using numerical data.

The status of several of the subspecies included here has been challenged by various authors for many reasons. The current trend in herpetology at the professional level is to recognize fewer and fewer subspecies on the basis that most populations of animals are more variable than normally believed if they could be adequately sampled over the entire range. Many subspecies, especially those of *Lampropeltis triangulum*, are based on small samples from only a few localities and possibly do not give an adequate idea of what the animals from an area really look like. Users of the following section should be warned in advance that many kingsnakes and milk snakes are not easily assigned to subspecies. This is also true of captive-bred specimens even from known stock because mutations and the narrow gene pool of the captive population often cause deviations in appearance and even meristics over just a few generations. Many freaks and sports of kingsnakes and milk snakes are now being bred either on purpose or by accident. Undoubtedly new populations of kingsnakes are yet to be found that will be thought by researchers to be worthy of description as new subspecies. The status of the three tricolored kingsnakes and of the species related to *L. mexicana* is also uncertain and not likely to be solved in the near future.

Genus *Lampropeltis* Fitzinger, 1843

The type species of the genus is *getulus* Schlegel. Synonyms often seen in older literature are *Ophibolus* Baird and Girard, 1853, also based on *getulus*, and *Osceola* Baird and Girard, 1853, based on *elapsoides*. The standard definition of the genus is as follows:

Maxillary teeth 12 to 20, solid, slightly increasing or slightly decreasing in size posteriorly, subequal, or the last two a little enlarged; mandibular teeth decreasing in size posteriorly; head not or but slightly distinct from neck; eye moderate, with round pupil; scales smooth, with two apical pits, in 17 to 27 rows; anal plate entire; tail moderate, subcaudals in two rows (Blanchard, 1921).

The eight species currently thought to comprise the genus can be recognized by the following key (modified from Blaney, 1973, and the literature). Actually, the first couplet involving teeth is unnecessary for hobbyists because the species of the two sections can be readily distinguished on sight after even slight familiarity with the genus.

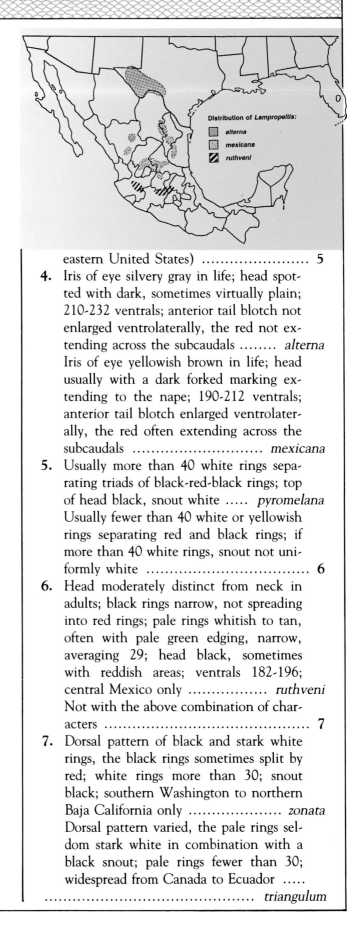

Distribution of *Lampropeltis*:
- alterna
- mexicana
- ruthveni

1. Posterior two maxillary teeth normal, not longer and stouter than more anterior teeth (*getulus* group) 2
   Posterior two maxillary teeth usually longer and stouter than more anterior teeth (*triangulum* group) 3

2. Dorsal background color light to dark, with darker dorsal and lateral blotches; scales without light centers ...... *calligaster*
   Dorsal background color usually dark, with light (yellow to white) crossbands, stripes, or spots at least laterally, some scales usually with light centers ..... *getulus*

3. Dorsal pattern usually of white-bordered gray bands or blotches alternating with black-bordered reddish saddles or rings; head relatively wide and distinct from neck; top of head spotted or with forked markings 4
   Dorsal pattern usually of rings of red, black, and yellow or white, red sometimes saddles or red rings missing; head usually relatively narrow and not very distinct from neck; top of head usually with black and white or red bands, rarely with forked markings (except in north-eastern United States) 5

4. Iris of eye silvery gray in life; head spotted with dark, sometimes virtually plain; 210-232 ventrals; anterior tail blotch not enlarged ventrolaterally, the red not extending across the subcaudals .... *alterna*
   Iris of eye yellowish brown in life; head usually with a dark forked marking extending to the nape; 190-212 ventrals; anterior tail blotch enlarged ventrolaterally, the red often extending across the subcaudals .... *mexicana*

5. Usually more than 40 white rings separating triads of black-red-black rings; top of head black, snout white ..... *pyromelana*
   Usually fewer than 40 white or yellowish rings separating red and black rings; if more than 40 white rings, snout not uniformly white 6

6. Head moderately distinct from neck in adults; black rings narrow, not spreading into red rings; pale rings whitish to tan, often with pale green edging, narrow, averaging 29; head black, sometimes with reddish areas; ventrals 182-196; central Mexico only .... *ruthveni*
   Not with the above combination of characters 7

7. Dorsal pattern of black and stark white rings, the black rings sometimes split by red; white rings more than 30; snout black; southern Washington to northern Baja California only .... *zonata*
   Dorsal pattern varied, the pale rings seldom stark white in combination with a black snout; pale rings fewer than 30; widespread from Canada to Ecuador .... *triangulum*

Gray Banded Kingsnake
Lampropeltis alterna (Brown, 1901)

The Gray Banded Kingsnake is a moderate-sized species about 4 feet (1.2 m) long with a very distinct head and an overall mottled gray color. Its pattern consists of a series of white-edged black blotches or saddles that may be red-centered. Alternating reduced markings may be present between the major markings. In the typical form (*alterna*) there are about 15-39 black saddles, while in the form *blairi* Flury, 1950, there are only 9-17 saddles. The eye is relatively large and has a silvery gray iris (a good character to separate it from *mexicana*). The ventral scale count is high for a member of the *mexicana* complex, 210-232. A more technical character helping separate this species from the very similar *mexicana* is that the proximal (lower) spines of the hemipenes are ovoid in cross section and approximately 0.7 mm long (shorter and more triangular in *mexicana*). Reaches a maximum size of about 50 inches (1.3 m).

RANGE: Southwestern Texas and northern Mexico (Coahuila, Durango). Specimens have been

A fairly typical example of *L. alterna* with a grayish background color and broad, unbroken red saddles. Photo by R. G. Markel.

collected over the entire Mapimian portion of the Chihuahuan Desert. These localities range from latitude 32°N to 25°N.

MERISTICS: Dorsal scale rows 25; ventrals 210-232; subcaudals 58-63; supralabials 7; infralabials 10-12; 9-39 saddles or rings.

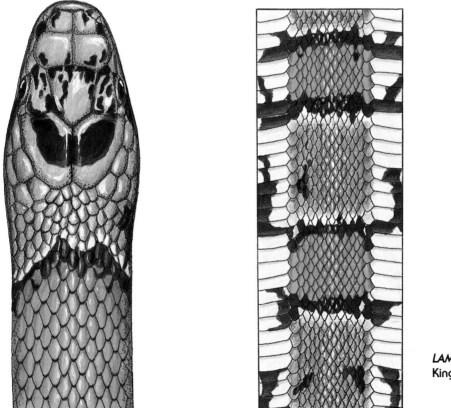

LAMPROPELTIS ALTERNA, Gray Banded Kingsnake

L. *alterna* and L. *mexicana* were long considered to be a single species known as the Mexican Kingsnake, and they have only recently been separated. These were among the first kingsnakes to be captive-bred in quantity. A hint of the many patterns found in these kingsnakes is visible here. Photo by K. Freeman.

HEAD PATTERN: Crown gray with black lines or dots; may be solid black.

DORSAL PATTERN: A series of white-edged black blotches or saddles or rings that may be red-centered at least in part; usually 14-20 saddles, but number extremely variable; between the saddles are grayish areas of background color often about the same width as the saddles. Alternative pattern may be a solid gray color with narrow black rings varying in number from 17-23; the rings may alternate with thin black bands that may be only a series of transverse dots; at times red may appear within the narrow black bands.

VENTRAL PATTERN: Light, almost white, with some bands of black nearly crossing the belly. Melanistic forms may have gray to dark gray or black dominating, especially under the tail.

JUVENILES: 7-10 inches (18-25 cm). Like the adults.

LENGTH: 42-50 inches (107-127 cm).

REVISIONS: Gehlbach, 1967; Garstka, 1982.

For many years L. *alterna* was called L. *blairi*, Blair's Kingsnake. This name was first used by Flury in 1950 for a seemingly new and very rare species from southwestern Texas, and it was almost 15 years before enough specimens had been collected to show that *blairi* was a variant of the also rare and poorly known L. *alterna*. The *blairi* form has broad red saddles, while the typical *alterna* has the red reduced or even absent. Photo by Ken Lucas, Steinhart Aquarium.

This exceptionally dark blue individual of *L. alterna* shows a fairly typical *blairi* pattern with some reduced red saddles posteriorly. Photo by R. W. Applegate.

Although most wild-caught *L. alterna* have grayish to blue-gray saddles, some individuals, both wild and captive-bred, have the gray accentuated into blue. Such individuals are especially striking. Photo by D. Soderberg.

In this specimen of *L. alterna* the red saddles are split with pale in the middle, producing an unusual effect more typical of some patterns of *L. mexicana*. The simple head pattern is more typical of *alterna*, however. Photo by Alex Kerstitch.

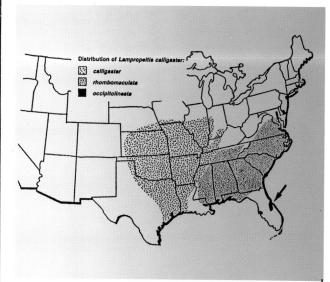

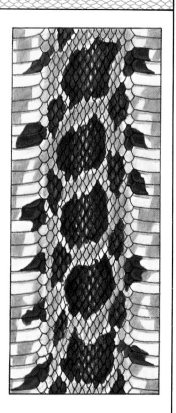

Prairie Kingsnake
Lampropeltis calligaster (Harlan, 1827)

In this relatively poorly known kingsnake the last two maxillary teeth are not enlarged (as in *L. getulus*). The dorsal pattern consists of a pale to dark brownish ground color with dark brownish to reddish dorsal and lateral blotches. The two subspecies are very variable in pattern and color with locality, age, and individual differences. The hemipenes are only slightly asymmetrical and shallowly bilobed. Two subspecies are usually recognized, but a third has recently been described and is here treated as a problematical form. In a survey of the literature, Fitch (1970) found the species to produce from 6 to 17 eggs per clutch with an average of 11. The species as a whole is distributed from Maryland

L. calligaster calligaster, juvenile. Photo by R. G. Markel.

LAMPROPELTIS CALLIGASTER CALLIGASTER, Prairie Kingsnake

and northern (or central) Florida west through Tennessee and Kentucky, Indiana, Illinois, and southern Iowa, to Nebraska, western Kansas, Oklahoma, and eastern Texas.
REVISIONS: Blanchard, 1921; Blaney, 1978.

Prairie Kingsnake
Lampropeltis calligaster calligaster (Harlan, 1827)

The nominate subspecies of the Prairie Kingsnake usually has about 60 dorsal blotches and 23-27 dorsal scale rows. As a general rule, the dorsal blotches have concave anterior and posterior margins, but this is quite variable. A variety of habitats are used by this kingsnake, including prairie, old fields, roadside embankments, cultivated fields, and open shrubby or wooded situations. Klimstra (1959) found that an Illinois population had a diet composed of 68.6% mammals, 11.2% amphibians, 6.8% reptiles, 6.8% birds, and 6.4% insects. Reaches a length of 50 inches (127 cm).

A darker specimen of *L. c. calligaster*. Such clean patterns are more typical of juveniles than adults. Photo by R. G. Markel.

RANGE: Indiana westward to Nebraska, south through the Mississippi valley to eastern Texas and western Louisiana.

MERISTICS: Dorsal scale rows 23-27, usually 25 or 27; ventrals 196-215; subcaudals 38-57; supralabials 7-8, usually 7; infralabials 9-11; dorsal blotches 46-78.

HEAD PATTERN: A V-shaped arrowhead on top; may be gray to deep olive gray without pattern or moderately heavily patterned with lines and spots.

The concave anterior and posterior margins of the dorsal blotches are quite obvious in this *L. c. calligaster*. Photo by R. G. Markel.

DORSAL PATTERN: About 60 reddish or greenish black-edged squarish middorsal blotches that usually have concave margins; may be split into two separate rows; usually two rows of smaller lateral spots or blotches. Pattern is rarely obscured except in very large adults. The spots occasionally fuse into stripes.

VENTRAL PATTERN: Normally yellow with square brown blotches.

JUVENILES: 9-11 inches (23-28 cm) at hatching. Usually strongly spotted.

LENGTH: 30-42 inches (76-107 cm).

Mole Snake
Lampropeltis calligaster rhombomaculata
(Holbrook, 1840)

The Mole Snake seldom has more than 56 dorsal blotches and 21-23 dorsal scale rows. As a general rule, if the dorsal blotches are visible they tend to have convex or straight anterior and posterior margins. This subspecies is noted for the loss of pattern in half-grown to large specimens, resulting in virtually plain brownish

LAMPROPELTIS CALLIGASTER RHOMBOMACULATA, Mole Snake

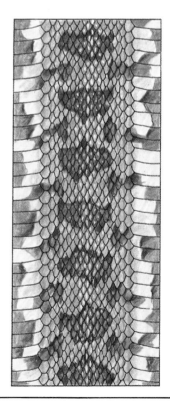

A virtually patternless adult *L. c. rhombomaculata.* Photo by R. G. Markel.

snakes. Habitats include woodlots, open fields, and cultivated areas. It is noted for its secretive, burrowing habits, specimens seldom being found except at night after heavy rains. Hamilton and Pollack (1955) found two individuals that contained cotton rats (*Sigmodon*). Lockwood (1954) noted a preference for snakes and glass lizards (*Ophisaurus*) in a captive individual from North Carolina. Adults reach 48 inches (122 cm).

RANGE: Maryland to northern Florida, west to Tennessee and southeastern Louisiana.

MERISTICS: Dorsal scale rows 19-23; ventrals 186-213; subcaudals 36-55; supralabials 7; infralabials 8-9; dorsal blotches 42-71, usually about 56.

HEAD PATTERN: Except in small specimens that may display a broken dark arrowhead, any pattern is obscured by the overall dark color.

DORSAL PATTERN: Usually about 56 reddish brown dark-edged middorsal blotches with straight to slightly convex margins; smaller blotches often present laterally. Older specimens may lack all pattern and be totally dark brown. Stripes may develop as a pattern anomaly.

VENTRAL PATTERN: Yellowish to whitish, checkered, spotted, or clouded with brown.

JUVENILES: 8-9 inches (20-23 cm) at hatching. Boldly marked with red or brown well-separated blotches. Two longitudinal brown stripes on neck.

LENGTH: 30-40 inches (76-102 cm).

South Florida Mole Snake [PROBLEMATICAL]
Lampropeltis calligaster occipitolineata Price, 1987

This newly described taxon is known from only three specimens and photos of a fourth, so it is not yet possible to evaluate its distinctiveness. It

A very typical Mole Snake. Photo by R. G. Markel.

seems to combine some of the characters of the other two subspecies in an unusual fashion. The two known localities are from 100 and 200 miles (160-320 km) south of the known range of *L. calligaster rhombomaculata* in northern Florida. It is distinguished by the high number of dorsal blotches (78-79) combined with 21 rows of dorsal scales.

RANGE: Known only from Okeechobee and Brevard Co., Florida.

MERISTICS: Dorsal scale rows 21; other scale counts presumably as in *L. calligaster rhombomaculata;* 78-79 dorsal blotches, still distinct in large adults.

A young Mole Snake with a relatively reduced dorsal pattern. Photo by R. Anderson.

HEAD PATTERN: Small blotches, dots, and fili-grees of dark lines on the crown.

DORSAL PATTERN: Dorsal blotches small, still visible in large adults.

VENTRAL PATTERN: Presumably as in the other subspecies.

JUVENILES: Unknown.

LENGTH: Presumably as in the other subspecies.

Common Kingsnake

Lampropeltis getulus (Linnaeus, 1766)

The Common Kingsnake ranges from the Atlantic coast of North American below the 41st parallel to the Pacific coast below the 43rd parallel, south to Zacatecas and San Luis Potosi, Mexico. This range also includes most of the Baja Peninsula. The species is seemingly absent within this area only from Colorado, the northern third of New Mexico, northeastern Arizona, and most of Utah and northeastern Nevada. In elevation it is found from sea level to about 6500 feet (1950 m). In much of this area it is a common and well-known snake, one of the few that is actually respected for its famous ability to prey on venomous snakes.

Because of the complex variation that occurs across its broad range, it is difficult to define the species in a meaningful way, although the overall dark brown to black background color, the absence of bright (i.e., red or tangerine) colors, and the strong tendency for at least some lateral scales to have yellow centers are usually sufficient for recognition. There are some 198-

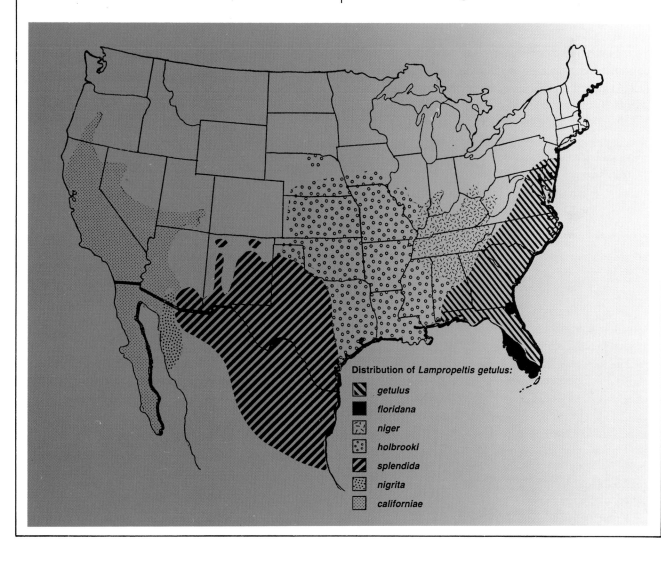

Distribution of *Lampropeltis getulus*:

- getulus
- floridana
- niger
- holbrooki
- splendida
- nigrita
- californiae

The amount of variation present in the California Kingsnake, *L. g. californiae*, has long confused herpetologists. Not only are there both ringed and striped phases, but each phase has variations in details of pattern and colors. This ringed phase snake is one of the most strikingly marked patterns, with rich yellow and chestnut rings. More typical of the *boylii* phase is a combination of blackish and whitish rings. Few individuals are as attractive as this one. Breeders strive to produce such remarkable patterns on a consistent basis. Photo by B. Kahl.

255 ventrals and 37-63 subcaudals. The hemipenes are distinctly to slightly bilobed. Nine subspecies were recognized in the latest revision, with some four or five other names still being used by hobbyists. These names are treated as problematical forms in the following discussion because they are currently being bred in captivity in pure form and the names are still in common use; they are probably synonyms of other subspecies as Blaney (1977) determined, and it might be better if their names were no longer used until new evidence is discovered to revalidate them.

D. R. Frost and J. T. Collins, in *Herpetological Review,* 19(4), Dec. 1988, have pointed out that technical nomenclatural rules require slight spelling changes in two taxa of this species: *getulus* becomes *getula,* and *niger* becomes *nigra.* Whether these changes will be accepted or disregarded is presently uncertain. The old spellings are retained here.

The California Kingsnake, the Florida Kingsnake (and its variants), and to a lesser extent some of the other subspecies are among the most commonly kept and bred snakes in North America. The California Kingsnake is famous for its dimorphic patterns, both white-ringed and white-striped individuals occurring with different frequencies in different parts of the range. Albinos are commonly bred of several of the subspecies. The number of eggs per clutch ranges from 5 to 17, with an average of about 10 (Fitch, 1970).

REVISION: Blaney, 1977.

California Kingsnake
Lampropeltis getulus californiae (Blainville, 1835)

In the California Kingsnake the ground color is black or brown and there are stripes or bands (rings) of white or cream. Specimens of both patterns occur sympatrically in southern California and Baja California, but over most of the range only the ringed form occurs. The status of Baja California specimens is still somewhat controversial, with the names *conjuncta* (Cope, 1861) and *nitida* Van Denburgh, 1895, being used for the banded or ringed (*conjuncta*) and striped or melanistic (*nitida*) forms. The typical banded or ringed form was long known as a separate species, *boylii* (Baird and Girard, 1853). *Yumensis* Blanchard, 1919, is a synonym of this subspecies and is based on ringed specimens from the Arizona area. Unusual variants are not uncommon in this

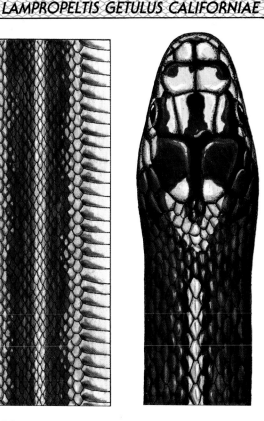

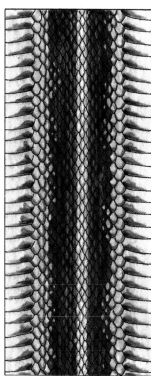

LAMPROPELTIS GETULUS CALIFORNIAE, California
Kingsnake (Striped Phase)

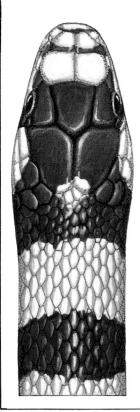

LAMPROPELTIS GETULUS CALIFORNIAE "BOYLII",
California Kingsnake (Ringed Phase)

subspecies, with specimens intermediate between the ringed and striped phases being recorded. Populations in the San Joaquin Valley may occur with amelanistic ventral scales. Albinos and sports are commonly bred.

The habitats used by this snake vary from desert to chaparral, farm land, river bottoms, grasslands, and deciduous and coniferous forests. Adults reach 60 inches (152 cm).

RANGE: Oregon to southern Utah, Arizona, Nevada, California, and the Baja Peninsula, Mexico. Intergrades with *splendida* in southeastern Arizona.

MERISTICS: Dorsal scale rows 23-25; ventrals 213-255; subcaudals 44-63; supralabials 7-8; infralabials 9-10; dorsal light crossbands (rings) 21-44 (sometimes striped).

HEAD PATTERN: Dark on top with a light spot at the center rear; snout paler, as is lower half of head.

DORSAL PATTERN: Two pattern types: banded or ringed, and striped; intermediate forms with broken stripes or spots, or even half-banded and half-striped. Dark brown or black with a white or

Two extreme specimens of the ringed California Kingsnake. Note the ventrolateral expansion of the white bands in the specimen above, a feature that is useful for distinguishing this subspecies from other black and white banded kingsnakes. Photo above by S. Kochetov, that below by Ken Lucas, Steinhart Aquarium.

A very cleanly striped specimen of *L. g. californiae*. Photo by R. G. Markel.

pale yellow pattern. In banded specimens the pale bands are distinctly widened ventrolaterally.
VENTRAL PATTERN: May be checkered or have bands crossing the belly. Occasionally with a completely black belly or just the undertail black.
JUVENILES: Normally copies of the parents, but banded and striped individuals may hatch from the same clutch.
LENGTH: 42-50 inches (107-127 cm).

Above: A very contrastingly patterned ringed phase of *L. g. californiae*. Photo by R. G. Markel.

This strangely patterned California Kingsnake has the dorsal pattern very irregular and has spotting on the sides below the bands. Perhaps it is from the intergradation area with *splendida*. Photo by Alex Kerstitch.

Two aberrant patterns of the striped phase of *L. g. californiae*. Aberrant patterns are not uncommon in certain populations of the California Kingsnake and can even be very constant within small geographical areas, with many or most individuals from a locality being distinguishable. The top specimen has the sides largely yellow, with a relatively constant row of middorsal diamonds. Such specimens clearly show the relationship of the ringed and striped phases. The bottom specimen shows a mixture of middorsal spots, broken stripes, and even a fairly complete band. Photo at top by R. G. Markel, that at bottom by B. E. Baur.

A dark, banded Baja California specimen of the "*conjuncta*" phase of the California Kingsnake. Photo by R. G. Markel.

The California Kingsnakes that occur in Baja California have long been a bone of contention among herpetologists and kingsnake breeders. They differ in small details from more typical *californiae* but usually are not accorded formal recognition by herpetologists, although there are at least two available names for kingsnakes from the region, "*conjuncta*" for banded specimens, and "*nitida*" for striped specimens. Baja kings have a strong tendency toward melanism, as shown here. In the top and center photos a barely visible middorsal pale stripe can just be seen on close inspection. The bottom photo is of a specimen that appears to lack an easily visible pattern. Breeders try to maintain pure lines of such variants both because they are popular with fanciers and because they are helping conserve small but distinctive populations that may eventually be recognized as valid taxa. Photos by R. G. Markel.

Florida Kingsnake
Lampropeltis getulus floridana Blanchard, 1919

The Florida Kingsnake is distinguished from other subspecies by having 22 to 66 light (yellow or orangish) crossbands on a chocolate-brown ground color. With age the background color lightens, resulting in pale centers to many scales. Northern populations have a tan background color with 12-20 dark brown saddles, but the colors lighten further south, the trend resulting in southern Florida specimens (the so-called *brooksi* Barbour, 1919, form) that have almost no dark pattern, being an overall very pale yellow because of the large number of light-centered scales.

Two varieties still treated as recognizable forms by hobbyists are considered by Blaney to be relics of intergradation between *floridana* and *getulus*. The Blotched Kingsnake, *L. getulus goini* Neill and Allen, 1949, is also known as the Chipola River Kingsnake. It generally has a light background color with 15-17 wide darker saddles. The saddles are brown with a light yellow spot in each of the scales. The belly is also the same buff or light brown color as the saddles with alternating dark patches. The head is mostly light except that the labials have

A fairly typical specimen of the Florida Kingsnake, *L. g. floridana*. Photo by G. Marcuse.

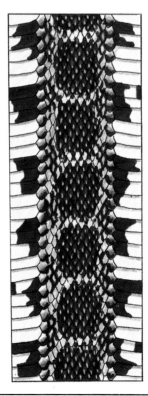

LAMPROPELTIS GETULUS FLORIDANA,
Florida Kingsnake

LAMPROPELTIS GETULUS FLORIDANA "BROOKSI", Florida Kingsnake (Golden Phase)

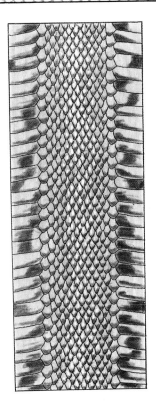

In this typical Florida Kingsnake the pale crossbands are distinct from the dark background color yet most of the dark scales are distinctly pale-centered. By increasing the extent and size of the pale spotting, the *"brooksi"* phase is produced. Photo by R. G. Markel.

This Florida Kingsnake shows the distinctive mahogany tint often associated with the subspecies. This is one of the more attractive subspecies of *getulus*. Photo by J. Coborn.

narrow reduced lines or dots. It has dorsal saddles that do not extend onto the belly as in *getulus* and has fewer saddles compared to the average number in the Eastern Kingsnake. Ventrals average 216, subcaudals 53, and there are 19-21 dorsal scale rows. The habitat includes sandy ground, natural springs, rivers, and wooded swamps at sea level as well as limestone hills. Adults reach 60 inches (152 cm). It is found only in the Chipola and Apalachicola River valleys of the Florida panhandle. Blaney synonymized it with *getulus getulus* and considered it to be an extreme of an intergrade *g. getulus* × *g. floridana* population. Its attractive and distinctive pattern makes it highly

The Blotched Kingsnake, *L. g. floridana* "*goini*", a juvenile (above) and two adults. This strikingly patterned snake is considered to be an individual variant of a relic *g. getulus x g. floridana* intergrade population, but it is highly regarded by breeders and kept in pure lines. Photos by R. G. Markel.

desirable to hobbyists and it is being bred as a pure form.

The Outer Banks Kingsnake, *L. getulus sticticeps* Barbour and Engels, 1942, is restricted to Ocracoke and probably other islands of the Outer Banks of North Carolina. It is distinguished by the broad, flat head heavily marked with white. Large white spots on the labials continue down the sides of the body. There are about 24 white crossbands that do not reach the ventrals. The ground color is dark brown, but the white lateral spots are very prominent. The belly is dark with light areas. Sandy ground with brush and more heavily wooded areas are inhabited. Adults reach about 50 inches (127 cm) in length. Blaney considered this form to be an intergrade between *getulus* and *floridana* although today it occurs well north of the range of *floridana*. The suggestion has been made that it is an isolated population preserving intergradation that occurred thousands of years ago when the ranges of the subspecies were different from the present ranges, *floridana* occurring more northerly along the coast.

RANGE: Central and southern Florida, with isolated populations in northeastern Florida and the Panhandle. Intergrades very broadly with *getulus* over much of north-central Florida, with typical examples (*brooksi* type) restricted to mostly the southern third of Florida.

MERISTICS: Dorsal scale rows 23; ventrals 210-221; subcaudals 44-58; supralabials 7-8; infralabials 9-10; light dorsal crossbands 22-66.

HEAD PATTERN: Scales light-centered, appearing darker at margins; labials pale with thin dark vertical lines.

In the Outer Banks Kingsnake, *L. g. getulus x floridana "sticticeps"*, the appearance is much as in typical *L. g. getulus* but there is a tendency to light-centered scales, prominent white spotting along the lower side, short middorsal crossbands, and slight differences in head shape. This has been a controversial taxon since its first description, with herpetologists taking different stands often based on different material that may or may not actually represent the taxon. Although herpetologists currently do not hold *"sticticeps"* to be valid, breeders are attempting to maintain the form in captivity. Photos by R. G. Markel.

DORSAL PATTERN: Base color brown with numerous yellow crossbands forming squarish saddles. Saddles do not encircle the body. In southern Florida the saddles and the background become indistinct as the scales all become yellow-centered, giving the entire body a very pale yellow color with only traces of darker brown on the scale edges.

VENTRAL PATTERN: Yellowish, checkered or blotched with dark brown; the pale areas may extend up the sides and are intersected with smaller dark blotches.

JUVENILES: 8-10 inches (20-25 cm). May have chain-like markings like *g. getulus*. Many dorsal scales have reddish brown centers and some along the sides show light centers.

LENGTH: 36-48 inches (91-122 cm).

Eastern Kingsnake
Lampropeltis getulus getulus (Linnaeus, 1766)

The Eastern Kingsnake is also often called the Chain Kingsnake because of the distinctive pattern of 15-44 light (usually yellow) crossbands on a chocolate-brown to black ground color; the crossbands usually are connected by a lateral row of fused yellow spots that produce the chain-like pattern. Woods, meadows, borders of creeks, and other aquatic edge habitats are used by this snake, which can be quite common in some areas. Hamilton and Pollack (1955) found that out of 13 specimens from Georgia, 11 had consumed reptiles and 2 had eaten mammals. Turtle, lizard, and snake eggs are also a frequent part of the diet. May reach 82 inches (208 cm) in length.

RANGE: Southern New Jersey to West Virginia, south to northern Florida, and west to the Appalachians and southeastern Alabama. Intergrades broadly with *floridana* in central Florida.

MERISTICS: Dorsal scale rows 21; ventrals 200-223; subcaudals 37-57; supralabials 6-8; infralabials 9-10; light dorsal crossbars 15-44.

HEAD PATTERN: Dark with light yellowish flecks; labials with dark vertical lines.

The Eastern Kingsnake is also known as the Chain Kingsnake because of the link-like pattern. It intergrades broadly with the Florida Kingsnake to the south, partially a result of changes in distribution since the last Ice Age. Photo by R. G. Markel.

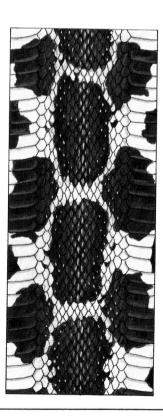

LAMPROPELTIS GETULUS GETULUS, Eastern Kingsnake

This young *L. g. getulus* shows a relatively large amount of red ventrolaterally and seems to have some paler dorsal scale centers. It possibly comes from within the extensive area of intergradation of *L. g. getulus* and *L. g. floridana*. Photo by Ken Lucas, Steinhart Aquarium.

DORSAL PATTERN: Black or dark brown with narrow yellow to cream crossbars connected to pale lateral bands to form chain-like links.

VENTRAL PATTERN: Predominantly dark with some small light scattered blotches.

JUVENILES: 9-11 inches (23-28 cm) at hatching. Duplicates of the parents but with the contrast usually greater and the pale colors brighter.

LENGTH: 48-60 inches (122-152 cm).

Speckled Kingsnake
Lampropeltis getulus holbrooki Stejneger, 1902

The Speckled Kingsnake, also known as the Salt-and-Pepper Kingsnake, has several distinct pattern types each considered by Blaney to represent microgeographic races. The subspecies is readily recognized by the bright brown to black ground color covered with numerous small yellow spots, usually one per scale, seldom forming distinctive crossbars; when crossbars are formed, they do not reach the sides. One pattern has uniform yellow spots on each scale and is typical of the Mississippi Valley bottomlands. The spots expand somewhat to form indistinct dorsal bands in the eastern Mississippi and western Alabama area, while populations from west of the Mississippi Valley from southern

LAMPROPELTIS GETULUS HOLBROOKI, Speckled Kingsnake

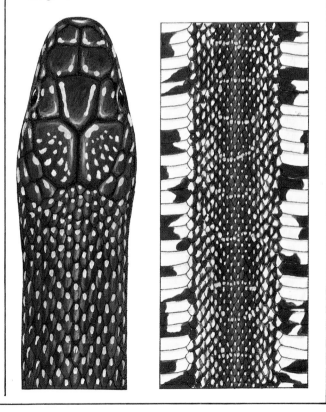

Iowa and western Illinois south to central Louisiana have very irregular spotting with a strong tendency to fuse into distinct narrow crossbars. The habitat used varies from upland woods to prairie. Adults reach 64 inches (163 cm)

RANGE: Southwestern Illinois to southern Iowa, south to eastern Texas and east to southwestern Alabama. Intergrades broadly with *niger* to the east and (especially broadly) with *splendida* to the west.

MERISTICS: Dorsal scale rows 21; ventrals 197-222; subcaudals 37-59; supralabials 6-8; infralabials 9-10; light dorsal crossbars absent or variably developed, 41-85 when present.

HEAD PATTERN: Dark, spotted with yellow.

DORSAL PATTERN: Dark brown or black, normally with a bright yellow spot in each scale. Spots may fuse to form short and narrow crossbars.

VENTRAL PATTERN: Belly cream with scattered dark squares and rectangles.

JUVENILES: 7-9 inches (18-23 cm) at hatching. With more of a tendency to crossbars than in typical adults, the pale scale centers developing with age.

LENGTH: 36-48 inches (91-122 cm).

Examples of the three types of dorsal patterns in the Speckled Kingsnake: top, uniformly spotted lowlands; center, distinctly crossbanded western; bottom, indistinctly crossbanded eastern. Photos by R. G. Markel (top and center) and S. Kochetov.

Black Kingsnake
Lampropeltis getulus niger (Yarrow, 1882)

The Black Kingsnake is, as the common and scientific names imply, mostly black. There may be a few pale-centered scales on the back, and occasionally short, narrow, weak crossbars may form by fusion of spots. Pale lateral spotting is not developed. Some individuals lack all pale markings. Habitats include old fields, open woods, stream edges, and a variety of habitats that have been disturbed by man. Adults may reach 56 inches (142 cm).

RANGE: Southern Ohio to southeastern Illinois south to central Alabama and northwestern Georgia. Intergrades broadly with *holbrooki* to the west.

MERISTICS: Dorsal scale rows 21; ventrals 198-217; subcaudals 39-55; supralabials 7; infralabials 9-10; at most 21-70 weak and narrow pale crossbars.

HEAD PATTERN: Black with scattered pale spots.

DORSAL PATTERN: Usually black above, without or with a faint pale pattern. If a pale pattern is developed, it usually consists of a few white to yellow spots on the back that may fuse into weak, narrow crossbars that do not reach the sides. Lateral scales without spots.

VENTRAL PATTERN: Belly usually about half and half black and white in no particular pattern.

JUVENILES: 7-8 inches (18-20 cm). A chain-like pale pattern may be very distinct at hatching but fades with growth.

LENGTH: 36-45 inches (91-114 cm).

A fairly typical *L. getulus niger*, the Black Kingsnake. Photo by G. Carlzen.

Even a very dark *holbrooki* (below) is much more patterned than a *niger*. Photos by G. Carlzen (above) and R. G. Markel.

LAMPROPELTIS GETULUS NIGER, Black Kingsnake

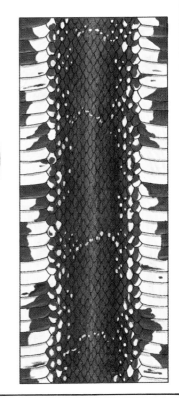

The Mexican Black Kingsnake usually lacks all yellow pattern. Photo by R. G. Markel.

Mexican Black Kingsnake
Lampropeltis getulus nigritus Zweifel and Norris, 1955

The Mexican Black Kingsnake is restricted in pure form to northwestern Mexico and is recognized by the uniformly black coloration occasionally relieved by a few small yellow spots

Only adult *L. t. gaigeae* are as uniformly black as *L. g. nigritus*. Photo by R. G. Markel of *nigritus*.

on the lateral scales and occasionally on a few dorsal scales; crossbars are not developed. This is a nocturnal desert snake about which little is known. Adults to 40 inches (102 cm).

RANGE: Western Sonora and northwestern Sinaloa, Mexico. Intergrades with *splendida* and *californiae* occur in southeastern Arizona.

MERISTICS: Dorsal scale rows 23-25; ventrals 213-225; subcaudals 47-56; supralabials 7-8; infralabials 9-10; pale dorsal crossbars absent.

HEAD PATTERN: Black.

LAMPROPELTIS GETULUS NIGRITUS, Mexican Black Kingsnake

DORSAL PATTERN: Uniformly dark brown to black, pattern absent. Weak pale centers may be developed in some lateral and dorsal scales.

VENTRAL PATTERN: Almost totally black.

JUVENILES: 7-8 inches (18-20 cm). Hatchlings differ from adults in having a faint pattern of pale crossbars.

LENGTH: 24-36 inches (61-91 cm).

Desert Kingsnake
Lampropeltis getulus splendida (Baird and Girard, 1853)

The Desert Kingsnake is a dark brown to black snake with the lateral scales heavily spotted with yellow. Usually almost every lateral scale has a yellow center. Yellow-centered scales may also occur on the back to form narrow pale crossbars that often connect with the pale lateral scales. The crossbars are numerous when present, 42-97. This is a nocturnal snake typical of dry, desert-like regions. It may increase in abundance in irrigated areas and in the vicinity of streams. Adults reach 60 inches (152 cm).

RANGE: Central Texas to southeastern Arizona, south to San Luis Potosi and Zacatecas, Mexico, west to Sonora and Santa Catalina Island in the Gulf of California. Intergrades broadly with *holbrooki* to the east and north, with intergrades occurring over most of Kansas and Oklahoma. Also intergrades with *nigritus* and *californiae* in southeastern Arizona and northern Sonora.

MERISTICS: Dorsal scale rows 23-25; ventrals 199-237; subcaudals 40-62; supralabials 7-8; infralabials 9-10; light dorsal crossbars may number 42-97 when present.

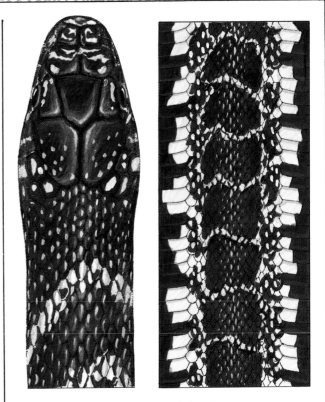

LAMPROPELTIS GETULUS SPLENDIDA, Desert Kingsnake

The many pale-centered lateral scales are typical of *L. g. splendida*. Photo by J. T. Kellnhauser.

In typical *splendida* the dorsal pattern consists of distinct dark blotches separated by yellow. Photo by R. G. Markel.

HEAD PATTERN: Black above, the labials pale with wide vertical lines.

DORSAL PATTERN: Dark brown or black, the lateral scales heavily spotted with yellow. Yellow-centered dorsal scales may be scattered or fused into narrow crossbars that often connect with the pale-centered lateral scales.

VENTRAL PATTERN: Predominantly black.

JUVENILES: 7-9 inches (18-23 cm). Back with squares of black separated by bright yellow crossbars.

LENGTH: 36-45 inches (91-114 cm).

A well-patterned *splendida* is a very pretty snake, but not all specimens are so distinctive. Photo by R. G. Markel.

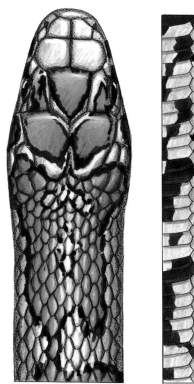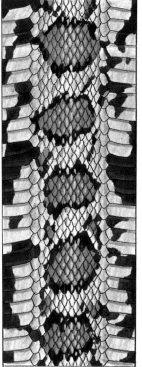

LAMPROPELTIS MEXICANA, San Luis Potosi Kingsnake

San Luis Potosi Kingsnake
Lampropeltis mexicana (Garman, 1884)

The San Luis Potosi Kingsnake, more commonly called the Mexican Kingsnake (although this concept also included *L. alterna*), is a moderate-sized species about 3 feet (1 m) long. It has a fairly distinct head and an overall mottled gray to yellowish or brown color with a pattern of white-edged black blotches, saddles, or rings that may be red-centered. Alternating reduced markings may be present ventrolaterally between the major markings. The anterior tail blotch is enlarged ventrolaterally and the red often extends onto or across the subcaudals (as opposed to *alterna*). The top of the head usually has a forked dark marking as opposed to the scattered spots and blotches of *alterna*. The iris of the relatively large eye is yellowish brown, not silvery gray as in *alterna*. The number of ventral scales varies from 190 to 212, lower than in *alterna*. The proximate spines of the hemipenes are rather triangular in cross section and only

 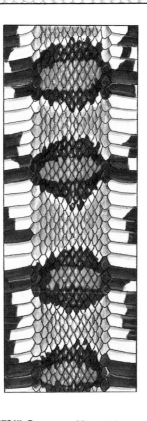

The width and shape of the dorsal blotches vary greatly in *L. mexicana*, with an appropriate number of synonyms and taxonomic confusion. This is a typical juvenile *mexicana*. Photo by R. G. Markel.

LAMPROPELTIS MEXICANA "GREERI", Durango Mountain Kingsnake

In the opinion of many, the San Luis Potosi Kingsnake includes varieties that are as colorful as any of the true tricolors. This hatchling exhibits a fairly typical pattern. Photo by R. G. Markel.

some 0.4 mm long. This species inhabits dry areas but not true deserts, often being found in dry pine-oak forests. It is nocturnal.

The taxonomy of this species is complex and all the problems are not yet solved. Because of complex individual and perhaps geographic variation in color and pattern, there are many synonyms, some of which still have their supporters. Included here are snakes formerly called *leonis* Guenther, 1893; *thayeri* Loveridge, 1924; and *greeri* Webb, 1961. Of these, *thayeri* and *greeri* are used by hobbyists for distinctive patterns that are kept in captivity.

The Durango Mountain Kingsnake, *L. mexicana greeri*, tends to have a light buff background color with a pattern of about 33 black or black-edged red bands narrowly bordered with white. None of the bands are interrupted middorsally at their widest point. The red of some posterior bands and the nuchal blotch are split with buff centers. The head lacks a black forked pattern (but interorbital bars are present); there instead is a distinct triangular or Y-shaped blotch on the neck that usually is very large. The ventral surface is mostly whitish with

The squarish dorsal saddles of a typical *mexicana* (above) contrast with the restricted saddles, often lacking red, that are found in many *"greeri"* (below). Photo above by R. G. Markel, that below by S. Tennyson.

The odd pattern of this *mexicana* resembles the form often called *"thayeri"* by hobbyists. Photo by Alex Kerstitch.

a few scattered black blotches. There may be an indistinct midventral pale stripe over part of the belly. Ventrals average 202, subcaudals 60. Adults are about 36 inches (91 cm) long. Specimens resembling this tend to come from the mountains of Durango, Mexico.

The Nuevo Leon Kingsnake is also known as the Variable Kingsnake, *L. mexicana thayeri.* As the name implies, it is exceedingly variable. In the same litter there may be some narrow-banded juveniles that resemble *L. alterna* and some that have red, black, and white rings like that of the Central Plains Milk Snake, *L. t. gentilis.*

This strangely patterned Durango Mountain Kingsnake has a reduced head pattern very closely resembling that of *L. alterna.* The innumerable patterns of these snakes are best kept as pure as possible by breeders. Photo by R. G. Markel.

Variations from black-bordered red blotches to narrow rings on a buff background to practically square saddles occur, yet there are also individuals with wide red bands bordered by black with cream between the black. The dorsal head marking is usually a black-bordered, anteriorly trilobed red blotch occupying adjacent parts of the frontal, prefrontals, parietals, and suboculars. It may be broken into separate spots, the black border may be diffuse or missing, or the head may be entirely black. (Specimens of typical *mexicana* have gray heads with darker dorsal and postocular markings.) Melanistic

The Variable or Nuevo Leon Kingsnake is perhaps the most confusing variation of *L. mexicana* because it occurs in virtually every possible pattern, including typically tricolored specimens. Photo by R. G. Markel.

forms are not uncommon. The red areas on the body extend laterally to the first or second scale row (row five in typical *mexicana*). Adults to about 36 inches (91 cm). Found on the eastern slope of the Mexican Plateau in the Miquihauna area of Tamaulipas.

The validity of these two forms is doubtful, and they have been synonymized with *mexicana* by Garstka and others. Admittedly, this species is too complex to understand the variation at this time.

Believe it or not, these radically different kingsnakes are siblings of *L. mexicana "thayeri"*. Photo by R. G. Markel.

RANGE: Principally the mountains surrounding the Saladan portion of the Chihuahuan Desert. Localities have ranged from 25°N in the Sierra Madre Oriental south to about 21°N. This includes portions of the Mexican states of Tamaulipas, San Luis Potosi, Coahuila, Nuevo Leon, Guanajuato, Zacatecas, and Durango.

MERISTICS: Dorsal scale rows 21-25; ventrals 190-211; subcaudals 51-65; supralabials 7; infralabials 8-11; dark dorsal blotches or bands 23-46.

HEAD PATTERN: Variable, but the nuchal blotch normally is present, is usually light-centered, and may be split into two or three forks; postocular dark stripe usually present.

DORSAL PATTERN: Variable, usually of white-edged saddles or blotches (sometimes rings) that may be red or brown at the center; blotches usually about 20-40.

VENTRAL PATTERN: Mottled dark and light; the saddles or rings may impinge from above.

JUVENILES: Highly varied from clutch to clutch, with captive-bred specimens representing all patterns and colors of the adults.

LENGTH: 24-36 inches (61-91 cm).

REVISIONS: Gehlbach, 1967; Garstka, 1982. See also Webb, 1961; Gehlbach and Baker, 1962; Gehlbach and McCoy, 1965.

L. p. infralabialis, the Utah Mountain Kingsnake. Photo by D. Soderberg.

Sonoran Mountain Kingsnake
Lampropeltis pyromelana (Cope, 1886)

The Sonoran Mountain Kingsnake is a snake of elevations between 2800 and 9100 feet (840-2730 m) where forests of pine, fir, pinyon

67

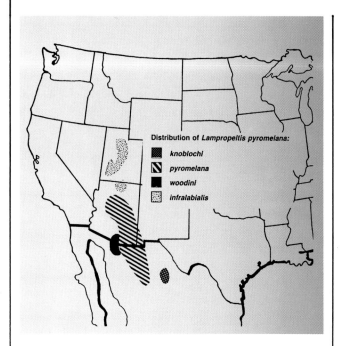

Distribution of *Lampropeltis pyromelana*:

- knoblochi
- pyromelana
- woodini
- infralabialis

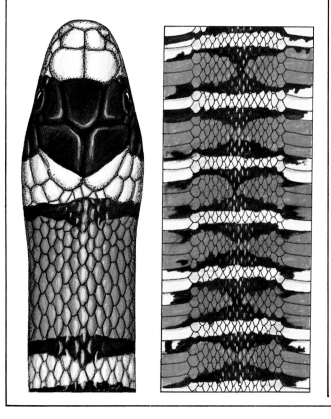

LAMPROPELTIS PYROMELANA INFRALABIALIS, Utah Mountain Kingsnake

juniper, or chaparral exist. Frequenting stream courses, this snake will feed on lizards and small mammals. The last two maxillary teeth usually are longer and stouter than the rest. The dorsal pattern consists of black-red-black triads separated by more than 40 white rings. The top of the head is black, with a uniformly white snout.

These little-known, small (30 inches, 76 cm), secretive snakes range from Utah and eastern Nevada south through Arizona and southwestern Mexico into northern Mexico. There are four subspecies currently recognized for the rather disjunct populations that comprise the species. REVISION: Tanner, 1953.

Utah Mountain Kingsnake
Lampropeltis pyromelana infralabialis Tanner, 1953

The Utah Mountain Kingsnake is a moderately slender snake with red, black, and white rings. There are only 9 infralabials (usually 10 in the other subspecies). This subspecies has a tendency for over half the white rings to be complete across the belly. There are 42-57 white rings on the body and 9-12 on the tail. This subspecies is rarely found below 5500 feet (1650 m) and usually is in leaf litter under pine and fir trees near permanent streams. Adults reach 40 inches (102 cm).

RANGE: Grand Canyon region of Arizona northward through central Utah and eastern Nevada.

MERISTICS: Dorsal scale rows 21-23; ventrals 213-230; subcaudals 59-79; supralabials 7-8; infralabials 9; white dorsal rings 42-57.

HEAD PATTERN: Snout white, rest of head black, the first white ring beginning on last third of head and encircling it.

DORSAL PATTERN: Half and sometimes more of white rings completely encircle the body. The red rings are widest and are bordered by black rings that often widen and connect across the red middorsally. The black rings often become so narrow laterally that they disappear before reaching the ventrals.

VENTRAL PATTERN: White rings often encircling the belly and sometimes narrowly bordered by black; rest of belly off-white to orangish where the red rings cross the belly and fade toward the center.

JUVENILES: 7-8 inches (18-20 cm). Much as in adults.
LENGTH: 30-36 inches (76-91 cm).

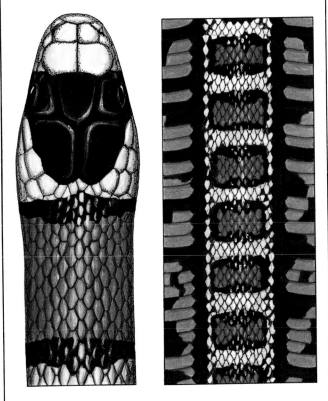

LAMPROPELTIS PYROMELANA KNOBLOCHI, Chihuahua Mountain Kingsnake

Chihuahua Mountain Kingsnake
Lampropeltis pyromelana knoblochi Taylor, 1940

The Chihuahua Mountain Kingsnake is a moderately slender snake occurring in northern Mexico. The white middorsal blotches are fused laterally into jagged white lateral bands completely isolating the reduced red saddles. This nocturnal and secretive snake is poorly known. Adults reach about 42 inches (102 cm) in length.

RANGE: Mojarachic region, Chihuahua, Mexico.

MERISTICS: Dorsal scale rows 23; ventrals 254-263; subcaudals 59-73; supralabials 7-8; infralabials 10; red dorsal saddles 70 or more.

HEAD PATTERN: Snout white, rest of head black, narrowing about eye; first white ring very wide, connecting with white from snout under eye.

Because of its limited distribution in a seldom-collected area, few typical specimens of the Chihuahua Mountain Kingsnake are in collections. Photo by R. G. Markel.

DORSAL PATTERN: White rings normally connected laterally into jagged bands. The red rings often are saddle-like and do not extend onto the ventrals. The red normally is not broken middorsally by the black rings.

VENTRAL PATTERN: Belly pattern variable, usually mostly black or white with narrow black bands that are not continuations of the dorsal black rings.

JUVENILES: Much as in the adults.

LENGTH: 36 inches (91 cm).

In this specimen of *L. p. knoblochi* the red saddles are not as distinctly cut off by black ventrally as is typical of the subspecies. Photo by R. G. Markel.

69

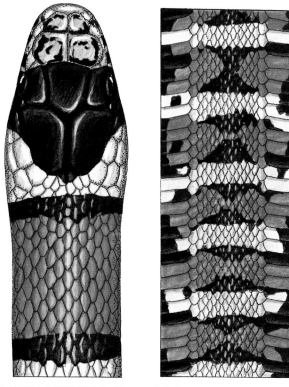

LAMPROPELTIS PYROMELANA PYROMELANA, Arizona Mountain Kingsnake

Arizona Mountain Kingsnake
Lampropeltis pyromelana pyromelana (Cope, 1886)

This moderately slender kingsnake has the rings of black separated by over 41 narrow white to buffy rings. The black rings usually are separated by scarlet rings but are not connected across the red middorsally. The head is black but the snout is white. There are 10 infralabials.

A very dark Arizona Mountain Kingsnake. Counts of rings are more important than colors in identification of this subspecies. Photo by R. S. Funk.

This subspecies, the most widely distributed, is found in wooded areas and is secretive. Adults reach 42 inches (107 cm).

RANGE: Chihuahua and Sonora, Mexico, north through central Arizona; not in the Huachuca Mountains.

MERISTICS: Dorsal scale rows 23; ventrals 214-228; subcaudals 61-75; supralabials 7-8; infralabials 10; white dorsal rings 42-61.

HEAD PATTERN: Snout white, rest of head black above; first white ring narrow and starting on last quarter of head.

DORSAL PATTERN: Over 41 white bands encircle the body and are bordered by thin black rings that usually do not connect middorsally across the red rings and also do not extend onto the ventrals. The red and white rings remain the same width as they descend to the ventrals.

VENTRAL PATTERN: White rings continue across the belly, separated by pale orange extensions of

In the typical *L. p. pyromelana* the black rings usually do not intrude greatly on the red rings middorsally. Note the use of the word *usually*. Photo by L. Porras.

the red rings and a few black blotches in no particular pattern.

JUVENILES: 7-8 inches (18-20 cm) at hatching. Like the adults.

LENGTH: 30-41 inches (76-104 cm).

Huachuca Mountain Kingsnake
Lampropeltis pyromelana woodini Tanner, 1953

The Huachuca Mountain Kingsnake has fewer white rings than does the adjacent Arizona Mountain Kingsnake, 37-40 vs. 42-61. Lizards

The counts of rings would identify this specimen as a *L. p. pyromelana X L. p. woodini* intergrade. Photo by S. Tennyson.

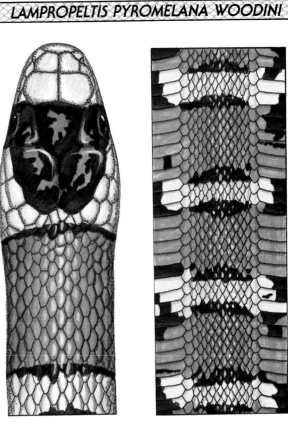

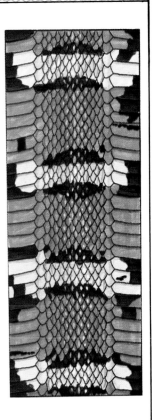

LAMPROPELTIS PYROMELANA WOODINI, Huachuca Mountain Kingsnake

A typical hatchling *L. p. woodini.* Photo by R. G. Markel.

The white snout of this hatchling Huachuca Mountain Kingsnake is one of the identifying characters of *L. pyromelana* and is constant for all the subspecies of the species. Photo by R. G. Markel.

and small rodents are its primary foods. Adults reach 44 inches (112 cm).

RANGE: Restricted to the Huachuca Mountains of southern Arizona and adjacent Mexico.

MERISTICS: Dorsal scale rows 23; ventrals 221-233; subcaudals 63-78; supralabials 7-8; infralabials 10; white dorsal rings 37-40.

HEAD PATTERN: Snout white, rest of head black; first white ring narrow above and wider below.

DORSAL PATTERN: Fewer than 42 white rings, these completely encircling the body. Black rings very narrow and fading out as they descend to the ventrals. Red rings continuing onto ventrals.

The adult *woodini* looks very similar in tone to an adult nominate *pyromelana* but has only 37 to 40 white rings on the body. Photo by Ken Lucas, Steinhart Aquarium.

LAMPROPELTIS RUTHVENI, Ruthven's Kingsnake

VENTRAL PATTERN: White and pale red rings completely encircling the body.
JUVENILES: 7-8 inches (18-20 cm). Like adults.
LENGTH: 36-42 inches (91-107 cm).

Ruthven's Kingsnake
Lampropeltis ruthveni Blanchard, 1920

Ruthven's Kingsnake is a problematical species only recently removed from the synonymy of *Lampropeltis triangulum*. It is still rare in collections and difficult to define. Although its relationships are with *L. mexicana*, it is superficially similar to the milk snakes in pattern. The head is distinct from the neck, as in *L. mexicana*, and the black rings tend to be outlined with a pale lime green, while the white rings have a tendency to become tan ventrolaterally. The white, red, and black rings are only two or three scale rows wide, and the black rings do not tend to encroach on the red rings middorsally. The top of the head is black, with some red or tan areas sometimes present.

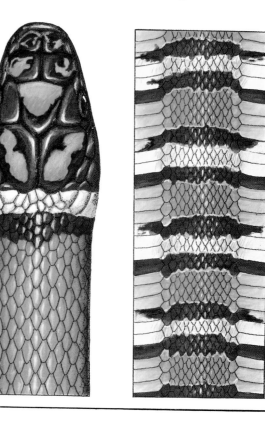

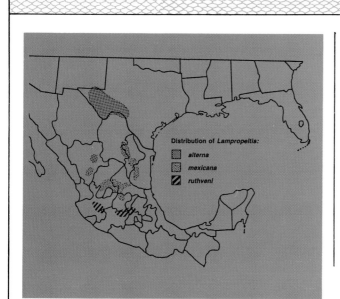

Distribution of *Lampropeltis*:

alterna

mexicana

ruthveni

There are only 182-196 ventrals, a lower count than for the sympatric subspecies of *L. triangulum*. This species has been collected from rocky, wooded uplands. Adults reach about 34 inches (84 cm).

RANGE: Mexican Plateau in Michoacan, Queretaro, and Jalisco. Perhaps more widely distributed.

MERISTICS: Dorsal scale rows 23; ventrals 182-196; subcaudals 49-57; supralabials 7-8; infralabials 8-9; white dorsal rings about 23-34.

HEAD PATTERN: Top of head black to parietals except for tan to reddish flecks and shading; white ring at back of head.

Ruthven's Kingsnake is probably the most poorly known kingsnake, only recently being taken out of synonymy with *L. triangulum*, and some authorities still doubt its validity. The broad head and barely visible pale green outlining of the darker bands indicate relationships with *L. mexicana*, as do the hemipenes. Photo below of hatchling by R. G. Markel.

The uniformly narrow black and white rings and the broad head with patches of red are hints that this is indeed a specimen of *L. ruthveni*, but only the ventral counts in combination with locality would be conclusive proof of the snake's identity. It is not impossible that there will be further changes in the status of this and other taxa related to *L. mexicana*. Photo above by D. Breidenbach.

DORSAL PATTERN: Ringed in white, red, and black. White and black rings about two scale rows wide, red rings about three scale rows wide. Black not splitting red rings middorsally. White rings may be shaded with tan laterally. Traces of lime green margins on black rings.

VENTRAL PATTERN: Rings extending around body, the red rings paler and the black rings sometime disappearing ventrally.

JUVENILES: Similar to adults.

LENGTH: About 28-32 inches (70-80 cm).

REVISION: Garstka, 1982. See also Blanchard, 1921.

*L. triangulum
annulata*, a typical
milk snake. Photo by
B. Kahl.

Milk Snake
Lampropeltis triangulum (Lacepede, 1788)

The Milk Snake is perhaps one of the most variable of snakes and is quite hard to define in such a way as to encompass all the variants. The last two maxillary teeth are longer and stouter than the preceding ones. The dorsal pattern is a combination of either brown, gray, and red dorsal blotches, or red, black, and yellow or white saddles or rings. The white to yellow rings (annuli) generally are fewer than 30 in number and usually are distinctly widened just above the ventrals. The head is not especially distinct from the neck in adults. In the ringed forms there is a strong tendency for the black rings to invade the red ones middorsally. Both vertebrates and invertebrates comprise the diet, with a general preference for small mammals and reptiles. Preference for a particular food item can vary greatly with each subspecies and possibly from one population to another. Fitch (1970) found clutch sizes to vary from 5 to 16, with a mean of about 10 eggs.

In the older literature the Milk Snake is often called *L. doliata*, a name now usually considered unidentifiable. There was much early confusion between the Milk Snake and the Scarlet Snake, *Cemophora coccinea*. (The Scarlet Snake has a much more pointed rostral scale and the belly is unmarked whitish, the red and black saddles of the back not encroaching on the belly.) The name Milk Snake derived from the belief that these snakes invaded barns and pastures to suck milk directly from the udder of the cow, an impossibility because of the structure of the teeth and throat of the snake.

Lampropeltis triangulum is one of the most widely distributed snake species, ranging from 48°N to nearly 4°S, a distance of almost 3600 miles (5760 km). The species ranges from southern Ontario and southwestern Quebec south through most of the United States east of the Rockies and also the Southwest, south through Central America into Colombia, Ecuador, and the Cordillera de la Costa of Venezuela. Milk Snakes are highly variable in size, pattern, and color, as well as habits and habitat. Many of the subspecies are poorly represented in collections and information on their natural history is poor to virtually

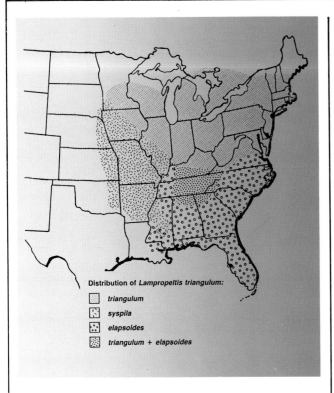

Distribution of *Lampropeltis triangulum*:

- triangulum
- syspila
- elapsoides
- triangulum + elapsoides

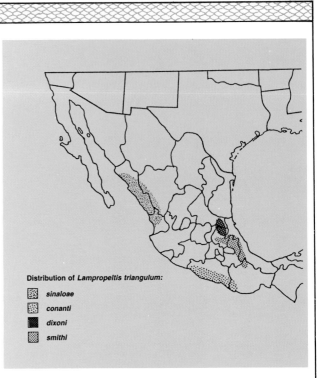

Distribution of *Lampropeltis triangulum*:

- sinaloae
- conanti
- dixoni
- smithi

nonexistent. Unless otherwise noted, the information following is based on Williams, 1978. It must be noted that several authorities feel that this species is greatly over-split and that the Central American snakes are much too variable and too poorly known to recognize so many subspecies. These authorities would prefer to use only the name of the species when

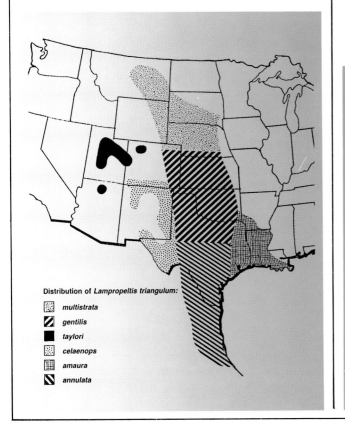

Distribution of *Lampropeltis triangulum*:

- multistrata
- gentilis
- taylori
- celaenops
- amaura
- annulata

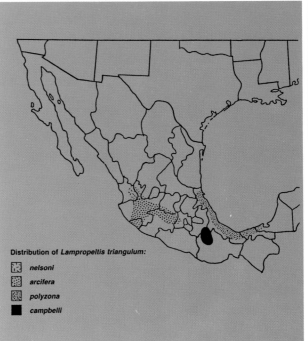

Distribution of *Lampropeltis triangulum*:

- nelsoni
- arcifera
- polyzona
- campbelli

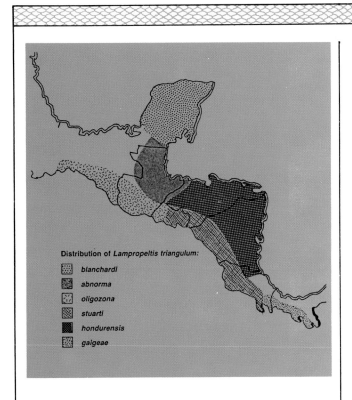

Distribution of *Lampropeltis triangulum*:

- blanchardi
- abnorma
- oligozona
- stuarti
- hondurensis
- gaigeae

referring to Central American specimens. Even in the United States it is often very difficult to separate individuals of the subspecies, and it is often suggested that they represent variation more in the nature of clines than actual subspecies. Do not expect to be able to identify Milk Snakes to subspecies in all instances even with good material, as the variation is sometimes exceedingly confusing. If the point of origin of the specimen is unknown, in many cases subspecies cannot be determined with certainty. REVISION: Williams, 1978. See also Quinn, 1983.

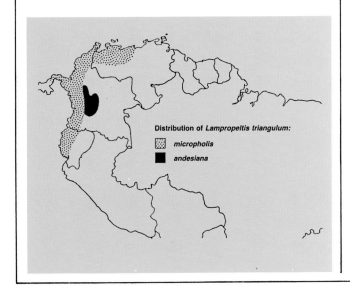

Distribution of *Lampropeltis triangulum*:

- micropholis
- andesiana

Guatemalan Milk Snake
Lampropeltis triangulum abnorma (Bocourt, 1886)

The Guatemalan Milk Snake has a broad white band on the snout. The white body rings are less than two scale rows wide, and the white scales are heavily tipped with black. The red rings are interrupted by black middorsally. This snake may live in a variety of habitats, reaching its greatest abundance in heavily forested areas. Adults reach 60 inches (152 cm).

RANGE: Northeastern Chiapas, Mexico, at least in the Laguan Ocotal area, eastward through the low and moderate elevations of central and northwestern Guatemala to northwestern Honduras.

MERISTICS: Dorsal scale rows 21-23; ventrals 219-234; subcaudals 50-61; supralabials 7-8; infralabials 8-11; red dorsal rings 20-31.

In this juvenile *L. t. abnorma* the black pigment is not as extensive as it will be in the adult and the whitish bands are relatively clean. Adults often have the black rings heavily encroaching on the red and whitish, crossing the red middorsally. Photo by S. Ballard.

HEAD PATTERN: Snout with a broad white band; rest of head black on top; first white ring encircles back of head, some black tips on the white scales.

DORSAL PATTERN: The rings have a tendency to completely encircle the body. The wider red rings range from 20-31, with an average of 25. The red scales may be black-tipped. There is black tipping on the scales of the white rings. The black-white-black ring combination is half the width of the red ring.

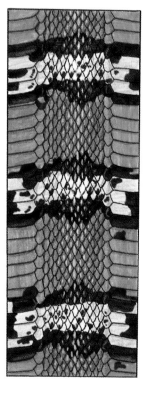

A note on the *triangulum* subspecies: Because the single species *L. triangulum* contains about half the total described taxa of the genus, the question often arises whether the currently recognized subspecies are "real" or totally artificial. Any user of this book is certain to recognize that the subspecies as a general rule closely resemble each other and replace each other geographically. Without careful counts of rings and ventral and subcaudal scutes from a fairly large series of specimens from known localities, it probably is impossible to correctly identify the subspecies of milk snakes. There often is extensive intergradation at the borders of the ranges, with one subspecies, such as *amaura*, intergrading with up to four other subspecies to produce a tremendous amount of variation.

LAMPROPELTIS TRIANGULUM ABNORMA, Guatemalan Milk Snake

VENTRAL PATTERN: Black and red rings totally encircle the body; the white rings on the belly have solid black patches.

JUVENILES: 8-10 inches (20-25 cm). The white areas appear brighter than in adults.

LENGTH: 48-60 inches (122-152 cm).

Louisiana Milk Snake
Lampropeltis triangulum amaura (Cope, 1861)

The Louisiana Milk Snake has a mostly red snout often heavily mottled with black and white, the remainder of the head black. The red rings are often separated from the ventrals by extensions of the black rings, so the red seldom crosses the belly; red rings number 13-21, broad. The pale rings are white to pale yellow. This mostly nocturnal snake inhabits hardwood lowlands and swamps as well as hilly terrain. Adults reach only 31 inches (79 cm).

This unusual variant of the Louisiana Milk Snake, *Lampropeltis triangulum amaura*, lacks the black pigment that usually colors the cap and the body bands. This gives the dark areas a chocolate tone that is very distinctive. Freaks such as this often can be bred successfully and maintained in the hobby. Photo by W. W. Lamar.

Subspecies with large ranges, such as *annulata, elapsoides, triangulum,* and *syspila,* often vary quite a bit within their ranges even without intergradation. For these reasons no attempt has been made to key out the subspecies of *triangulum* or to arrange them in any order that might possibly imply relationship. For the hobbyist, it is best to consider any milk snake without accurate locality data to be at best doubtfully identified. This is especially true with specimens from captive-bred lineages that may no longer be identical to wild specimens. Several authorities have expressed doubt as to the validity of the Central American subspecies, which certainly are confusing and virtually impossible to identify from a few specimens. Caution using subspecific names is strongly advised.

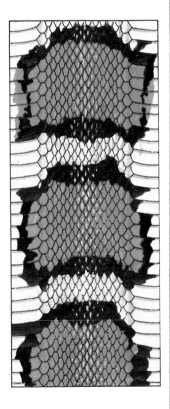

LAMPROPELTIS TRIANGULUM AMAURA, Louisiana Milk Snake

RANGE: Southern Arkansas and southeastern Oklahoma to the Gulf Coast of Texas and Louisiana.

MERISTICS: Dorsal scale rows 21; ventrals 171-201; subcaudals 39-55; supralabials 7; infralabials 8-10; red dorsal rings 13-25.

HEAD PATTERN: Head mostly black, the reddish snout mottled with black and white.

DORSAL PATTERN: 13-25 broad red rings, the rings extending onto the belly or stopping above the ventrals, in which case they appear to be saddles; red surrounded by black. Yellow bands widen ventrolaterally.

VENTRAL PATTERN: Belly largely yellowish, with some intrusion of the red and black bands into the area; black blotches also may be present.

JUVENILES: 5-6 inches (12.5-15 cm). Much like the adults, the yellow often white.

LENGTH: 16-22 inches (41-56 cm).

The amount of red on the snout of the Louisiana Milk Snake is individually variable. Although most individuals have reddish or mostly reddish snouts, some have only a reddish tan shade or a few spots of red. Because this subspecies intergrades broadly with four other subspecies on its borders, variation must be expected. Photo by W. W. Lamar.

LAMPROPELTIS TRIANGULUM ANDESIANA, **Andean Milk Snake**

The Andean Milk Snake is one of the two southernmost *Lampropeltis*, being restricted to the Andes Mountains of Colombia. As in the other southern milk snakes, it is large by milk snake standards and tends to be dark. Photo by D. Breidenbach.

Andean Milk Snake
Lampropeltis triangulum andesiana Williams, 1978

The Andean Milk Snake has a white snout with black scale margins. There are at least 24 red rings, and the red scales may or may not be tipped with black. Elevation records for this

L. t. andesiana. Photo by W. W. Lamar.

In this male *andesiana* the red scales are heavily tipped with black, as are the whitish scales. The amount of black varies in what seems to be an individual way in this subspecies. Photo by W. W. Lamar.

subspecies range from 733-9000 feet (220-2700 m). Adults reach 56 inches (142 cm).
RANGE: The Andes Mountains in Colombia.
MERISTICS: Dorsal scale rows 19; ventrals 218-227; subcaudals 40-47; supralabials 7-8; 8-9 infralabials; red dorsal rings 24-37.

HEAD PATTERN: Snout white, with narrow black scale edgings; head mostly white, with black flecking.

DORSAL PATTERN: Red rings range from 24 to 37, with an average of 31. The red scales may have fine black tips. The white scales are heavily black-tipped. The red rings are interrupted by black and are the same width as the black-white-black ring combination.

VENTRAL PATTERN: All the rings cross the belly; the white rings may contain black blotches.

JUVENILES: 8-10 inches (20-25 cm). Like the adults.

LENGTH: 45-54 inches (114-137 cm).

Mexican Milk Snake
Lampropeltis triangulum annulata (Kennicott, 1861)

The Mexican Milk Snake has a black head and snout. The first red ring is interrupted by black ventrally. The scales of the red and yellow rings are not tipped with black. The red rings number from 14 to 20. This snake inhabits semiarid habitats from sea level to 4000 feet (1200 m).

The Mexican Milk Snake is one of the more widely distributed subspecies, extending from southern Texas over much of northeastern Mexico. It intergrades widely with *gentilis* to the north and is often difficult to identify with certainty. As a rule the mostly black head and the extensively black ventral surface will distinguish it. The colors may be relatively dull and subdued or very bright. This is one of the more often-seen wild-collected milk snakes available in the hobby. Photo by R. G. Markel.

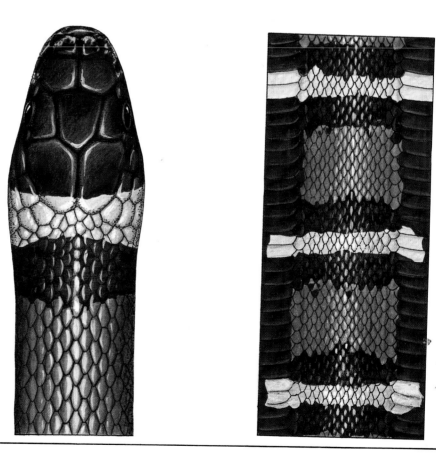

LAMPROPELTIS TRIANGULUM ANNULATA, Mexican Milk Snake

This colorful specimen of the Mexican Milk Snake has the black rings relatively narrow and not encroaching on the red rings middorsally. Notice the extensively black head. Photo by Ken Lucas, Steinhart Aquarium.

During the warmer summer months it is nocturnal. Adults are about 30 inches long (76 cm).

RANGE: Extreme southern Texas southward to southern Tamaulipas and westward to central Nuevo Leon and southern and eastern Coahuila.

MERISTICS: Dorsal scale rows 21; ventrals 181-207; subcaudals 42-56; supralabials 7-8; infralabials 9; red dorsal rings 14-20.

HEAD PATTERN: Head and snout black.

DORSAL PATTERN: The red rings, 14-20 in number, are slightly broader than the black-yellow-black ring combination. The red rings do not cross the belly. The black rings are relatively wide and encroach heavily on the red rings middorsally.

VENTRAL PATTERN: Belly mostly black with some red and yellow, the yellow rings crossing the belly.

JUVENILES: 7-8 inches (18-20 cm). Like the adults.

LENGTH: 24-30 inches (61-76 cm).

Jalisco Milk Snake
Lampropeltis triangulum arcifera (Werner, 1903)

The snout of the Jalisco Milk Snake is black, sometimes with white flecks. The first black ring may touch the angle of the jaws. The red and

At first glance *L. t. arcifera* resembles *annulata*, but the belly is largely red and there are more red rings. Photo by R. S. Funk.

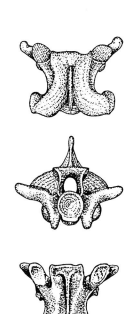

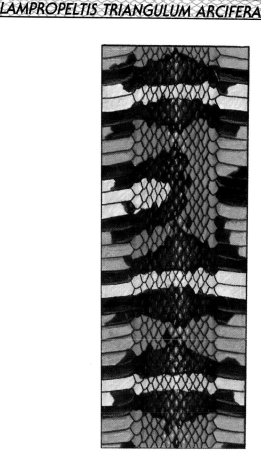

Lampropeltis similis (lower two figures), the probable ancestor of *L. triangulum,* is known from only a few vertebrae. Its vertebrae are quite different from those of *L. getulus* (top two figures). After Holman, 1964, in part.

LAMPROPELTIS TRIANGULUM ARCIFERA, Jalisco Milk Snake

white scales are not tipped with black. The number of red rings varies from 14 to 31. One individual was found to contain six juvenile mice of the genus *Reithrodontomys.* Habitats include arid tropical scrub, mesquite grasslands, and pine-oak forests. Elevations vary from 2300-11600 feet (700-3500 m). Adults reach a maximum length of about 42 inches (107 cm).

RANGE: In general, this subspecies inhabits the Mesa Central of Mexico, excluding the eastern portion. It occurs in Morelos southward into extreme northern Guerrero, in central Michoacan in the Lake Patzcuaro area, in south-central Jalisco around Lake Chapala, and in the more arid regions of western Queretaro. Possibly it also occurs in southwestern Puebla and western Hidalgo.

MERISTICS: Dorsal scale rows 21; ventrals 192-217; subcaudals 43-54; supralabials 7-8; infralabials 7-8; red dorsal rings 14-31.

HEAD PATTERN: Snout and rest of head black, the snout sometimes with small white flecks.

DORSAL PATTERN: Red body rings range from 14 to 31, with an average of 22. Red and white ring scales are not black-tipped. The black and white rings are about the same width, and the black rings do not taper toward the ventrals.

VENTRAL PATTERN: Black pigment interrupts the red and white rings ventrally.

JUVENILES: 8-9 inches (20-23 cm). Like adults.

LENGTH: 36-42 inches (91-107 cm).

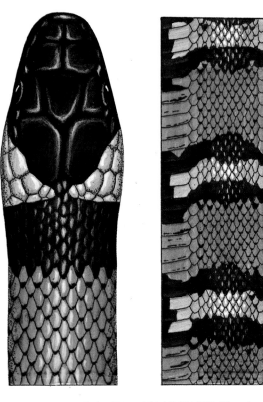

LAMPROPELTIS TRIANGULUM BLANCHARDI, Blanchard's Milk Snake

L. t. blanchardi is the milk snake of the Yucatan Peninsula. In specimens with well-developed color patterns the bright yellow rings contrast strongly with the red and black, especially on the sides of the nape, where a bright golden yellow triangle often develops. Photo by D. P. Muth.

HEAD PATTERN: Head and snout black.
DORSAL PATTERN: The red rings average 17 and have scales tipped with black. The white scales may or may not be tipped with black. The red rings are not very wide, about the same as the black-white-black ring combination.
VENTRAL PATTERN: The black rings cross the belly, as do the white rings. There are black patches in the white rings.
JUVENILES: 8-9 inches (20-23 cm). Patterned like adults.
LENGTH: 36-42 inches (91-107 cm).

Blanchard's Milk Snake is one of the less commonly seen Central American milk snakes. Few are bred in captivity. Photo by D. P. Muth.

Blanchard's Milk Snake
Lampropeltis triangulum blanchardi Stuart, 1935

Blanchard's Milk Snake has a black head and snout with the first black ring complete ventrally and frequently connected middorsally to black pigment on the parietals. The red scales are distinctly tipped with black. The red rings number 14-20. This nocturnal snake occupies the deciduous forest zone of Yucatan and the rain forest of Quintana Roo and Campeche. Adults reach 42 inches (107 cm).
RANGE: The Yucatan Peninsula, including Yucatan, eastern Campeche, and Quintana Roo, Mexico.
MERISTICS: Dorsal scale rows 21-23; ventrals 206-224; subcaudals 47-58; supralabials 7-8; infralabials 8-9; red dorsal rings 14-20.

LAMPROPELTIS TRIANGULUM CAMPBELLI, Pueblan Milk Snake

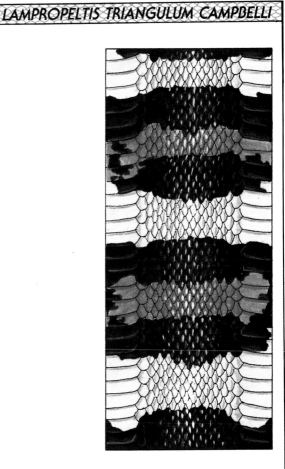

The broad white rings and white-mottled snout of *L. t. campbelli* are distinctive. Photo by S. Tennyson.

Pueblan Milk Snake
Lampropeltis triangulum campbelli Quinn, 1983

The Pueblan Milk Snake has a black snout with white speckling forming a mottled area that involves portions of the internasals, most of the prefrontals, and the anterior edge of the frontal. It curves across the frontal, forming a U. The average body rings are 16 red-orange, 32 black, and 16 white. The tail averages 5 black and 5 white bands with no red-orange bands. The white body rings are long but are slightly shorter at midbody than on the first dorsal scale row. About half the red rings are incomplete ventrally. Black tipping is absent from the white scales. This subspecies is at home in arid environments and can be found at elevations from 4935-5544 feet (1495-1680 m).

RANGE: Southern Puebla westward to eastern Morelos and south to northern Oaxaca, Mexico.
MERISTICS: Dorsal scale rows 21-23; ventrals 196-220; subcaudals 40-49; supralabials 7-8; infralabials 7-9; red-orange dorsal rings 14-22.

The Pueblan Milk Snake is a recently described subspecies that still is poorly known and generally is unavailable. It is now being captive-bred in small quantities. Of all the Mexican and Central American subspecies, it is one of the most easily recognized, at least in pure form. Photo by S. Tennyson.

HEAD PATTERN: Snout black. Head black with a light U on frontal. First white ring wider than at midbody.

DORSAL PATTERN: Number of red-orange rings on body 16, wide; tail averages 5 white and 5 black bands, no red. White rings at midbody wide, but not as wide as the first ring and lacking black tipping. Black rings wide, about same width as white at midbody.

VENTRAL PATTERN: About half of red rings complete across belly; rest of belly with continuations of white and black rings.

JUVENILES: 7-8 inches (18-20 cm). Like adults.

LENGTH: 28-36 inches (71-91 cm).

New Mexico Milk Snake
Lampropeltis triangulum celaenops Stejneger, 1903

The New Mexico or Big Bend Milk Snake has a mottled black and white snout and the remainder of the head is black. The black rings are expanded middorsally but do not fuse completely across the red rings, which number 17 to 25. The red and white scales are not black-tipped. This subspecies inhabits gamma grass areas, pinyon juniper woodlands, and oak forests at elevations up to 6900 feet (2090 m). Lizards (*Sceloporus*) are its chief food, up to six having

LAMPROPELTIS TRIANGULUM CELAENOPS, New Mexico Milk Snake

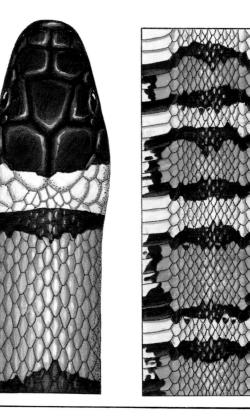

The pale rings of *L. t. celaenops* vary from white to pale yellowish tinged with tan. Photo by R. G. Markel.

been reported from one individual. Adults reach 24 inches (61 cm).

RANGE: The Rio Grande drainage of eastern New Mexico and southwestern Texas.

MERISTICS: Dorsal scale rows 21; ventrals 179-194; subcaudals 40-53; supralabials 7-8; infralabials 7-9; red dorsal rings 17-25.

The New Mexico Milk Snake is one of the plainer subspecies of *triangulum*, the colors usually appearing faded. It inhabits one of the dryer regions of North America, one with extreme climates. Photo by R. G. Markel.

HEAD PATTERN: Snout black, with or without white mottling; rest of head black.

DORSAL PATTERN: Black rings widened at midbody but do not cross red rings. Red rings average 22 on body. Yellow rings appear muddy because of brown flecking.

VENTRAL PATTERN: White bands widen as they cross belly. Midventral region mostly without black pigment.

JUVENILES: 7.5-11 inches (19-28 cm). Like adults but colors brighter.

LENGTH: 14-24 inches (36-61 cm).

Conant's Milk Snake
Lampropeltis triangulum conanti Williams, 1978

Conant's Milk Snake has a black snout and head to the middle of the parietals. The first black ring begins 1.5-3 scale lengths posterior to

In Conant's Milk Snake the colors often are vivid, the golden yellow bands being greatly restricted laterally. This is one of the rarely seen milk snakes. Photo by D. Beckwith.

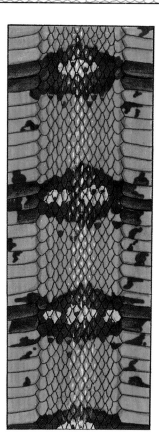

LAMPROPELTIS TRIANGULUM
CONANTI, Conant's Milk Snake

the parietals; it is incomplete ventrally or is narrowly connected across the first ventrals. Red scales are usually moderately black-tipped; white scales lack black tipping. The red rings number 11 to 20. This subspecies inhabits tropical lowlands near the coast but also occurs in highlands more interiorly. In the Chilpancingo area of Guerrero, this snake occupies the lower pine-oak and tropical deciduous forests. Adults to 46 inches (117 cm).

RANGE: The Sierra Madre del Sur in Guerrero and Oaxaca, Mexico.

MERISTICS: Dorsal scale rows 21; ventrals 196-221; subcaudals 45-57; supralabials 7-8; infralabials 7-10; red dorsal rings 11-20.

HEAD PATTERN: Snout and head black.

DORSAL PATTERN: Scales of red rings slightly to moderately tipped with black or may lack black. Red rings average 16. White rings usually with

black scale tipping. White rings narrow, the black rings wider than the white. The red rings are as wide as the black-white-black ring combination.

VENTRAL PATTERN: Rings cross belly, the white and red rings with black blotching.

JUVENILES: 8-9 inches (20-23 cm). Like adults.

LENGTH: 40-46 inches (102-117 cm).

Dixon's Milk Snake
Lampropeltis triangulum dixoni Quinn, 1983

Dixon's Milk Snake has a black snout with the black ending on the posterior half to fourth of the parietals. The first and subsequent red rings are narrow. The rings on the body are mostly black, the red and yellowish white rings narrow and with black-tipped scales. There are about 20

In Dixon's Milk Snake the black is extensive both dorsally and ventrally, and the dorsal red bands are often completely split middorsally by black. In pure form this subspecies occupies only a small range. Photo by D. Breidenbach.

red rings on the body and 5 yellowish bands on the tail. All the red rings are incomplete ventrally and many are incomplete dorsally (broken by black), a character helping distinguish the subspecies from its relatives. Poorly known.

RANGE: Mountain passes and valleys from southern San Luis Potosi into the Jalapan Valley of northeastern Queretaro.

LAMPROPELTIS TRIANGULUM DIXONI, Dixon's Milk Snake

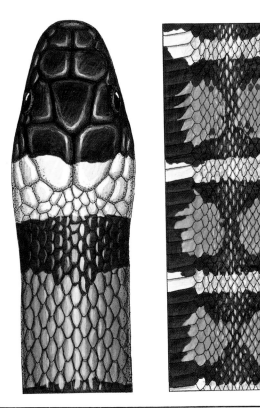

MERISTICS: Dorsal scale rows 21; ventrals 189-201; subcaudals 45-53; supralabials 7-8; infralabials 7-9; red dorsal rings 20-22.

HEAD PATTERN: Head and snout black.

DORSAL PATTERN: 20 red rings, the first two shorter than the rest. The body rings are mostly black, the red and yellowish white rings narrow. The red rings are heavily infiltrated with black and often completely divided middorsally.

VENTRAL PATTERN: Black rings and most of whitish rings complete around the body. No red on belly at least midventrally.

JUVENILES: 8-9 inches (20-23 cm). Black heavy, as in adults.

LENGTH: 36-42 inches (91-107 cm).

Scarlet Kingsnake
Lampropeltis triangulum elapsoides (Holbrook, 1838)

A Scarlet Kingsnake, *L. t. elapsoides*. Photo by R. G. Markel.

Northern specimens of Scarlet Kingsnakes tend to have narrower yellow bands than southern specimens. This southern specimen not only has broad yellow bands, it also has extensive middorsal encroachment of black through the red bands. Photo by F. J. Dodd, Jr.

 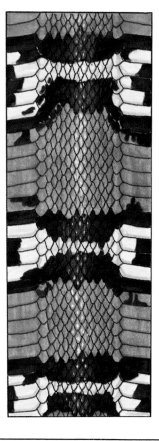

LAMPROPELTIS TRIANGULUM ELAPSOIDES, Scarlet Kingsnake

This specimen of the Scarlet Kingsnake is more typical of average individuals. Note the very regular band width and the bright red cap extending well behind the eyes.

The Scarlet Kingsnake is one of the most distinctively patterned subspecies of the Milk Snake. It has a red head with a black line across the posterior portion of the parietals. The body pattern consists of rings that normally are all complete across the belly. The red rings number 12-22. The red and white scales lack black tipping. This small (maximum length 27 inches or 69 cm) snake is a very good mimic of the coral snake *Micrurus fulvius*, with which it occurs, and is mostly nocturnal. Preferred habitats are pine and mixed woods. Food includes small mammals, lizards, snakes, and earthworms.

The exact status of this form is still uncertain, as it is sympatric with another subspecies, *L. t. triangulum*, in the Tennessee River valley of eastern Tennessee, the Cumberland Plateau of south-central and eastern Kentucky, and the eastern edge of the Appalachian Mountains in Macon Co., North Carolina and adjacent Georgia. Although it acts like a full species in this area, on the Piedmont and Coastal Plain of the Atlantic coast it intergrades with *L. t. triangulum* (intergrades were formerly called *temporalis* (Cope, 1893) and *virginiana*

In this juvenile *L. t. elapsoides* the pale bands are still solid white. In most milk snakes the bands tend to darken with age, so young specimens usually have whiter bands than older specimens, which are more likely to have bright yellow bands. Photo by R. Anderson.

In general appearance, Scarlet Kingsnakes are excellent mimics of the coral snake *Micrurus fulvius*. Photo by R. G. Markel.

Blanchard, 1920, names no longer in use).

These two subspecies are quite distinct from each other, and actually also very distinct from most of the other subspecies. The Scarlet Kingsnake is a small snake that feeds mainly on lizards and snakes, while the Eastern Milk Snake is larger and tends to feed on rodents. Because of these differences in size and food, and many differences in color pattern and counts, some authorities still prefer to consider the Scarlet Kingsnake a full species, regarding the areas of intergradation as due to habitat disturbance by man.

RANGE: Northern Virginia to Florida, inland to Tennesse, southern Kentucky, and Mississippi.

MERISTICS: Dorsal scale rows 17-19; ventrals 152-194; subcaudals 32-51; supralabials 7; infralabials 7-10; red dorsal rings 12-22.

HEAD PATTERN: Head red, with a narrow black line usually present across the posterior part of the parietals.

DORSAL PATTERN: Red rings bright or dull, numbering 12-22, with an average of 16. In the southern part of the range the black rings are wider and may intersect the red rings middorsally. The white or yellow rings are also wider in the southern part of the range.

VENTRAL PATTERN: All rings continue across the belly, the white rings expanding to become wider than the black.

JUVENILES: 5-8 inches (12.5-20 cm). Like adults.

LENGTH: 14-20 inches (36-51 cm).

Black Milk Snake
Lampropeltis triangulum gaigeae Dunn, 1937

This is a melanistic subspecies, or at least it tends toward melanism. The head and body pattern in large adults is obscured by black pigment. Juveniles and young adults may retain some pattern. The red rings number 17 to 22 when visible. Habitats include wet or moist forests at relatively high elevations, 5000-7400 feet (1500-2220 m) in Costa Rica and 4300-6500 feet (1290-1950 m) in Panama. A large snake, adults reaching 5 feet (152 cm).

Except for the golden skin appearing between the scales, adults of *L. t. gaigeae* are solid black. It has been suggested that the development of black pigments in this subspecies is a method of helping control body temperature. Photos by S. Tennyson.

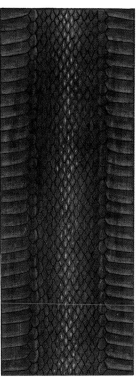

LAMPROPELTIS TRIANGULUM GAIGEAE, Black Milk Snake

The young Black Milk Snake is ringed with red, black, and yellow as in typical milk snakes. It is only when adulthood is reached that more and more black pigment is developed. Large adults may show no trace of pattern through the black. Photo by R. S. Funk.

RANGE: The mountains of Costa Rica and Panama.

MERISTICS: Dorsal scale rows 19; ventrals 216-236; subcaudals 42-63; supralabials 7-8; infralabials 8-10; red dorsal rings (if visible) 17-22.

HEAD PATTERN: White may cross snout in juveniles; rest of head black.

DORSAL PATTERN: Large adults uniformly black. Juveniles and young banded in red, black, and yellow.

VENTRAL PATTERN: Adults dull grayish below except under chin paler.

In general appearance *gaigeae* closely resembles *stuarti*, the subspecies found just to the north, but the meristics are different. Photo by R. S. Funk.

JUVENILES: This is the only known subspecies with different patterns as a juvenile and adult. Hatchlings 9-10 inches (23-25 cm). Red body rings 17-22, with narrow yellow rings bordered by black. The red and yellow scales are usually slightly to moderately tipped with black. Rings are complete across the belly, with some black flecks in the red.

LENGTH: 54-60 inches (137-152 cm).

Central Plains Milk Snake
Lampropeltis triangulum gentilis (Baird and Girard, 1853)

The Central Plains Milk Snake has a black snout mottled with white. The rest of the head is black, with white flecks between the eyes. Normally the red rings are interrupted midventrally by black and some may be crossed by black middorsally as well. There are from 20

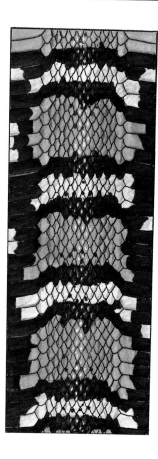

*LAMPROPELTIS TRIANGULUM
GENTILIS*, Central Plains Milk Snake

The black snout heavily mottled with white and the faded colors usually serve to identify the Central Plains Milk Snake. Photo by R. G. Markel.

to 32 red rings on the body, 26 to 38 total. The pale areas tend to be yellowish. Habitat varies from prairie to pine and deciduous forests. Adults to 36 inches (91 cm).

RANGE: Western half of Oklahoma, eastern Colorado, the Texas Panhandle, south-central and southwestern Nebraska, and central and western Kansas.

MERISTICS: Dorsal scale rows 21; ventrals 181-209; subcaudals 40-51; supralabials 7-8; infralabials 8-10; red dorsal rings 20-32.

HEAD PATTERN: Snout black, mottled with white (may be sulfur yellow); rest of head black except for some white flecks between the eyes.

DORSAL PATTERN: 25-40 yellowish rings. The yellow and black rings may or may not be broken midventrally or middorsally. Red rings often crossed by black, especially middorsally along the posterior portion of the body. Red rings 20-32 on the body.

VENTRAL PATTERN: Red rings broken by black midventrally; black and yellow rings cross belly.

LAMPROPELTIS TRIANGULUM HONDURENSIS, Honduran Milk Snake

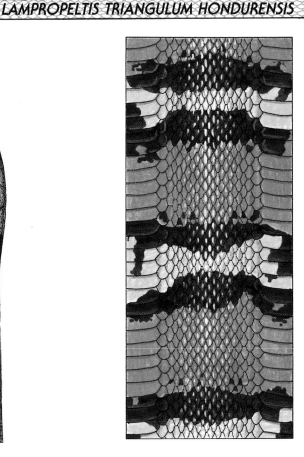

JUVENILES: 6-8 inches (15-20 cm). Like adults, but pale rings often bright white.
LENGTH: 30-36 inches (76-91 cm).

Honduran Milk Snake
Lampropeltis triangulum hondurensis Williams, 1978

The Honduran Milk Snake has a broad yellowish band on the snout reaching to the posterior border of the internasals and most of the prefrontals. The rest of the head is black to the posterior fourth of the parietals. Red-orange scales lack black tipping or are slightly tipped. Red rings number 14-26. This snake inhabits low to moderate elevations, specimens having been collected between 40 and 400 feet (12-120 m). Adults reach 48 inches (122 cm).

RANGE: Caribbean slope of Honduras (except the northwest), Nicaragua, and probably northeastern Costa Rica.
MERISTICS: Dorsal scale rows 21-23; ventrals 216-221; subcaudals 49-61; supralabials 7-8; infralabials 8-10; red dorsal rings 13-26.
HEAD PATTERN: Snout with a broad yellowish band; rest of head black.

The typical form of the Honduran Milk Snake is a strikingly patterned but quite typical Central American milk snake. There is little black tipping of the red and yellow bands, and the yellow snout band is large. Photo by R. S. Funk.

Three variants of the Honduran Milk Snake, *L. t. hondurensis*. The typical snake (lower right) has bright yellow bands in strong contrast to the bright red bands. In some specimens the yellow bands are greatly obscured with red to produce a bright orange that still is distinct from the red (lower left). Finally, in the "tangerine" morph (above) the red and yellow bands are the same shade of deep red-orange and not distinguishable. A few individuals of the "tangerine" even have the black bands reduced. Photos by S. Kochetov (above), R. S. Funk (lower right), and Guido Dingerkus (lower left).

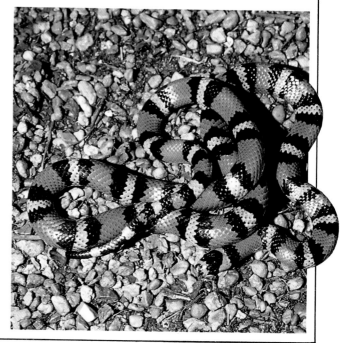

DORSAL PATTERN: Red rings on body 13-26, average 17. Red scales lack black tipping or are very slightly tipped. Some individuals lack yellow rings and may be overall very dark or overall bright tangerine red. Yellow rings narrow at best, with black tipping on the scales. Red rings twice as wide as the black-yellow-black ring combination

VENTRAL PATTERN: Black, yellow, and red rings entirely circle the body.

JUVENILES: 8-10 inches (20-25 cm) at hatching. Like adults.

LENGTH: 40-48 inches (102-122 cm).

Ecuadorian Milk Snake
Lampropeltis triangulum micropholis (Cope, 1861)

This very large subspecies has a pale snout with relatively narrow black areas anteriorly and posteriorly. The supralabials usually are white with black posterior edges. The remainder of the head is black to the middle or the posterior third of the parietals. Red scales are unmarked or black-tipped. The white to yellowish scales are extensively tipped with black. The red rings number 10 to 18 on the body. The Ecuadorian Milk Snake occupies the coastal plain, foothills, and lower mountains, while the higher elevations of the Andes are avoided. Adults reach 72 inches (183 cm), making it the largest form of the species.

RANGE: From the Canal Zone and eastern Panama south to south-central Ecuador (excluding

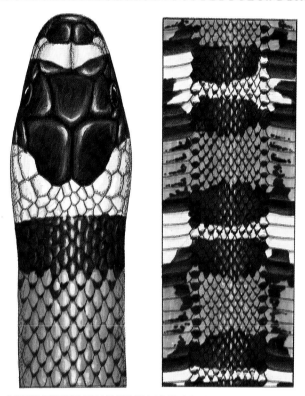

LAMPROPELTIS TRIANGULUM MICROPHOLIS, Ecuadorian Milk Snake

the high elevations of the Andes), east to the Rio Magdalena Valley of Colombia and as far as the Cordillera de la Costa of Venezuela.

MERISTICS: Dorsal scale rows 21; ventrals 209-229; subcaudals 39-51; supralabials 7-8; infralabials 8-10; red dorsal rings 10-18.

HEAD PATTERN: Snout whitish with black anterior and posterior margins.

Although very similar at first glance to the Andean Milk Snake, the Ecuadorian Milk Snake has the yellow scales on the head not outlined with black and has fewer red rings. It is a snake of the lowlands, while the Andean Milk Snake has a restricted range in the peaks. Photos of the Colombian form by S. Ballard.

DORSAL PATTERN: Red body rings wide, 10-18, averaging 14. Red scales unmarked with black or slightly tipped. White to yellowish rings wide, almost the same as red rings, with extensive black tipping.

VENTRAL PATTERN: Red rings encircle the body and enclose black flecks. Black rings continue across the belly, but the white rings are interrupted and replaced by black ventrally. Narrow white bands may occur as continuations of the black rings.

JUVENILES: 10-12 inches (25-30 cm). Like adults.

LENGTH: 60-72 inches (152-183 cm).

Pale Milk Snake
Lampropeltis triangulum multistrata
(Kennicott, 1861)

The Pale Milk Snake has an orange snout flecked with black. The head is black on the parietals and the posterior edge of the frontal and supralabials. The first black ring is incomplete, not crossing the venter; the other black rings are narrow. The red rings of other Milk Snakes are orangish here and short, not crossing or even reaching the venter; often they are reduced to saddles or blotches; the orange markings number 22-32. The venter has scattered black blotches. This Milk Snake inhabits the high plains of Nebraska, South Dakota, Wyoming, and Montana. Adults reach about 30 inches (76 cm).

Frost and Collins *(Herp. Review,* 19(4), Dec., 1988) have pointed out that the correct spelling of this taxon should be *multistriata.* It is not yet certain if this change will be accepted or fought.

RANGE: Central and northern Nebraska north to southwestern North Dakota and west to central Wyoming and southeastern Montana.

MERISTICS: Dorsal scale rows 21; ventrals 186-204; subcaudals 42-55; supralabials 7-8; infralabials 8-10; orange dorsal rings 22-32.

HEAD PATTERN: Snout light orange with scattered black flecks; rest of head black.

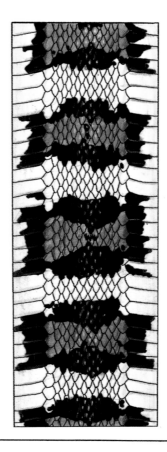

LAMPROPELTIS TRIANGULUM MULTISTRATA, Pale Milk Snake

The Pale Milk Snake is indeed pale in color, with the reds bright orange and the black greatly reduced. Often the red bands are mere saddles that do not reach the ventral scales. Photo by D. Breidenbach.

DORSAL PATTERN: Orange rings incomplete ventrolaterally, often just saddles or blotches, 22-32. Pale rings yellowish, complete. Black rings reduced.

VENTRAL PATTERN: Belly unmarked or nearly so, may have a few black flecks.

JUVENILES: 6-8 inches (15-20 cm). Like adults.

LENGTH: 24-30 inches (61-76 cm).

of the localities, Tres Marias Island, is covered with tropical deciduous forest that supports the majority of the population. However, in the coastal regions of Jalisco and Colima it occurs in areas where there is less rainfall. Mainland populations inhabit the northwestern portion of the Sierra Madre del Sur and the lower elevations of the western edge of the Mesa

A laying female of Nelson's Milk Snake. The status of this subspecies is quite uncertain as it occurs in pure form in only a very restricted area and produces apparent intergrades over a large area. Photo by D. Soderberg.

Nelson's Milk Snake
Lampropeltis triangulum nelsoni Blanchard, 1920

Nelson's Milk Snake has a white snout with scattered black pigment from the mid-prefrontals anteriorly; the rest of the head is black. The first black ring usually is more than one scale length posterior to the angle of the jaw and generally is incomplete or narrowly connected across the throat. The red and white scales are not tipped with black. Red rings number 13-18. Little is known about the habitats of this subspecies. One

Central. Adults to 42 inches (107 cm).

RANGE: Southern Guanajuato west through central Jalisco (avoiding the higher elevations) to the Pacific coast, then south through the coastal areas of Colima and onto the narrow coastal plain of northwestern Michoacan to Tres Marias Island. The status of many populations is uncertain as they may represent intergrades with other subspecies.

MERISTICS: Dorsal scale rows 21-23; ventrals 204-231; subcaudals 42-51; supralabials 7-8; infralabials 9-10; red dorsal rings 13-18.

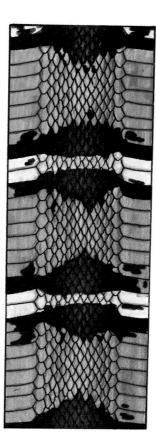

LAMPROPELTIS TRIANGULUM NELSONI, Nelson's Milk Snake

HEAD PATTERN: Snout white, may have a small amount of black pigment; rest of head black.

DORSAL PATTERN: Red body rings range from 13 to 18, averaging 16; scales with no black tipping. White ring scales also without black; rings narrow, as are the black rings. Red rings twice as wide as the black-white-black ring combination. All rings encircle body. Black rings do not enter red rings dorsally.

VENTRAL PATTERN: Completely ringed in red, white, and black.

JUVENILES: 8-10 inches (20-25 cm). Like adults, but rings purer white.

LENGTH: 36-42 inches (91-107 cm).

In both color pattern and meristics *L. t. nelsoni* closely agrees with *L. t. sinaloae*, with which it intergrades to the north. The average red body rings are only twice as wide as the black-white-black ring combination in *nelsoni*, three times in *sinaloae*. Photo by D. Soderberg.

LAMPROPELTIS TRIANGULUM OLIGOZONA, Pacific Central American Milk Snake

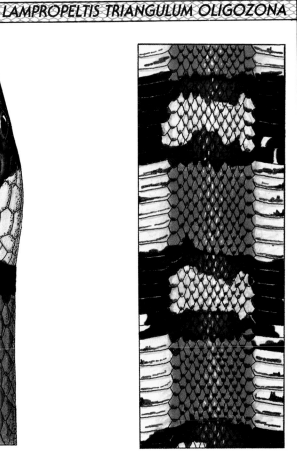

Pacific Central American Milk Snake
Lampropeltis triangulum oligozona (Bocourt, 1886)

L. t. oligozona has a black head and snout extending to the posterior fourth or fifth of the parietals. The first black ring starts half to three scale lengths posterior to the parietals, is complete across the venter, and usually extends onto two rows of gular scales. Red and white ring scales are distinctly tipped with black, and the white rings are occasionally obscured with black. Red rings number 10 to 16. This subspecies has been collected on the coastal plain and in adjacent hills at or below 1650 feet (500 m). It may follow river valleys and invade higher elevations. Adults may reach 42 inches (107 cm).

RANGE: Pacific slope from the village of Tehuantepec in Oaxaca, east and south along the coast and adjacent foothills of Chiapas, Mexico, and Guatemala.

MERISTICS: Dorsal scale rows 21–23; ventrals 221–234; subcaudals 52–61; supralabials 6–7; infralabials 8–10; red dorsal rings 10–16.

Identification of *L. t. oligozona* is difficult or perhaps impossible for the hobbyist. Like at least six or seven other Mexican and Central American milk snakes in general appearance, the subspecies differs from its nearest neighbors only in details of pattern and averages of counts. The distinct yellow snout wedge, black-tipped red and yellow scales, and tendency to restrict or obscure the white rings with black help in identification. Photo by W. W. Lamar.

HEAD PATTERN: Head and snout black.

DORSAL PATTERN: 10 to 16 red rings. Red and white ring scales distinctly tipped with black. White rings very narrow, sometimes absent due to encroachment of black pigment. Black rings often cut off white rings ventrolaterally.

VENTRAL PATTERN: Red rings do not extend onto belly, but are replaced by white. The black rings cross the belly and also replace the white rings ventrally.

JUVENILES: 8-10 inches (20-25 cm). Like adults.

LENGTH: 36-42 inches (91-107 cm).

Atlantic Central American Milk Snake
Lampropeltis triangulum polyzona (Cope, 1861)

This subspecies has a narrow light band crossing the snout near the prefrontal-internasal margin; the rest of the head is black. The first black ring begins on the parietal or not more than half a scale length posteriorly. Usually one or more black blotches occur ventrally in the red

LAMPROPELTIS TRIANGULUM POLYZONA, Atlantic Central American Milk Snake

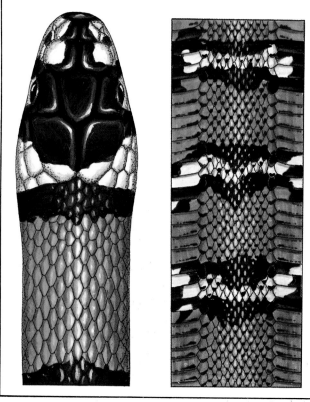

Again we have a virtually unidentifiable subspecies with few or no obvious characters. The snout has a yellow band that may be broken and the red and yellow rings are tipped with black, as in several other subspecies. Photo by D. Soderberg.

rings, but they rarely split the red. Red rings number 16 to 22. *L. t. polyzona* lives in the lowland tropical rain forests along the Gulf coast in San Luis Potosi, Veracruz, and Jalisco, Mexico, although it has been collected at 6000 feet (1800 m) at Volcan San Martin, Veracruz. Adults reach 60 inches (152 cm) in length.

RANGE: Coastal plain and foothills of Veracruz, extending up the river valleys into eastern San Luis Potosi, southward into the isthmus region, where the range broadens, and further east into Tabasco.

MERISTICS: Dorsal scale rows 21-23; ventrals 202-235; subcaudals 50-62; supralabials 7-8; infralabials 8-9; red dorsal rings 16-22.

HEAD PATTERN: Snout black with a narrow white band; rest of head black.

DORSAL PATTERN: Red body rings 16-22, the red scales heavily tipped with black. White rings indistinct, the scales heavily tipped with black. The narrow white rings are about half the width of the black rings, and the red rings are double the width of the black-white-black ring combination.

Well-marked specimens of *polyzona* are very pretty, but this is another seldom-seen milk snake that is not often available. Hobbyists should exercise caution when attempting to identify any Mexican or Central American milk snake as they form a puzzle of interdigitating populations with few obvious differences. Photo by R. G. Markel.

VENTRAL PATTERN: White rings cross belly and have black blotches in them; the white rings alternate with black rings that have white blotches in them. The red rings also extend onto the belly.
JUVENILES: 9-11 inches (23-28 cm). Like adults.
LENGTH: 54-60 inches (137-152 cm).

Sinaloan Milk Snake
Lampropeltis triangulum sinaloae Williams, 1978

The Sinaloan Milk Snake has a black head and snout with varying amounts of white mottling on the rostral, internasal, nasal, and loreal. The first black ring touches the angle of the jaw or is less than one scale length behind, forming a V on the throat. Red scales are not tipped with black. The black body rings are 2 to 2½ scales long. All rings completely encircle the body. Specimens are frequently found below 3300 feet (1000 m). The range coincides with the Pacific Coastal Lowland physiographic region. They can be found abundantly around the edges of cornfields. Adults reach 48 inches (122 cm).

RANGE: Southwestern corner of Sonora southeastward through the coastal plain and foothills of Sinaloa to near the southern border of Nayarit, and up to the Rio Fuerte into southwestern Chihuahua, Mexico.
MERISTICS: Dorsal scale rows 21-23; ventrals 205-228; subcaudals 46-60; supralabials 7-8; infralabials 7-10; red dorsal rings 10-16.
HEAD PATTERN: Snout black with white mottling; rest of head black.
DORSAL PATTERN: First black ring crosses the throat to form a V. Red body rings 10 to 16. All rings encircle body uniformly. Red scales not black-tipped, but white scales are. Red rings about three times as wide as black-white-black ring combination.
VENTRAL PATTERN: Black and white rings cross venter without interruption. Red rings also cross but may have some black blotches midventrally.
JUVENILES: 9-10 inches (23-25 cm). Pattern as uniform as in adults.
LENGTH: 40-48 inches (102-122 cm).

LAMPROPELTIS TRIANGULUM SINALOAE, Sinaloan Milk Snake

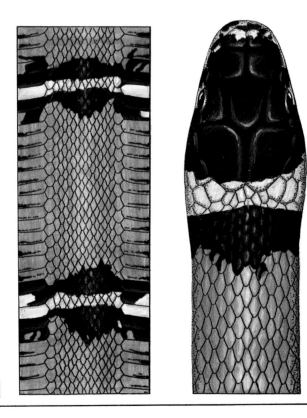

Although it was described only as late as 1978, the Sinaloan Milk Snake has become one of the most common and greatly prized of the tricolored kings. It is relatively easy to breed in captivity and has dropped significantly in price over the last few years. Photos on these pages by R. G. Markel (above) and B. Kahl (below and facing page).

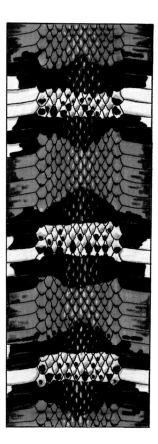

LAMPROPELTIS TRIANGULUM SMITHI,
Smith's Milk Snake

Smith's Milk Snake
Lampropeltis triangulum smithi Williams, 1978

Smith's Milk Snake has a black and white snout with the anterior portion of the internasals, prefrontals, nasals, loreals, and preoculars white and the posterior portions black. The first black ring starts at the posterior edge of the parietals or one or two scale lengths posteriorly. Red scales lack black tipping or are tipped with black. The white scales have a moderate amount of black tipping. The red body rings number 19 to 30. Dry tropical forests and coastal plains are inhabited by this Milk Snake. Adults reach 42 inches (107 cm).

RANGE: The Sierra Madre Oriental from southeastern San Luis Potosi southward through eastern Queretaro, Hidalgo, northeastern Puebla, and into the Jalapa area of Veracruz, Mexico.

The heavily white-mottled snout of *L. t. smithi* is fairly distinctive among Mexican milk snakes. The subspecies superficially resembles *annulata*, found to the North. Photo by D. Breidenbach.

Smith's Milk Snake is another example of a Neotropical milk snake that has few truly distinctive pattern features and must be separated by counts based on series from known localities. In the opinion of some experts this group of snakes is heavily over-split, with too many named subspecies representing slightly divergent populations. Photo by D. Breidenbach.

MERISTICS: Dorsal scale rows 21; ventrals 204-225; subcaudals 45-62; supralabials 7-8; infralabials 8-10; red dorsal rings 19-30.

HEAD PATTERN: Snout black and white; top of head black, the labials white barred with black.

DORSAL PATTERN: Red body rings number 19 to 30 and encircle the body. Red and white scales moderately black-tipped. White rings half as wide as black rings, the red rings narrower than the black-white-black ring combination.

VENTRAL PATTERN: All rings cross the belly uniformly; red rings with scattered black pigment ventrally.

JUVENILES: 8-9 inches (20-23 cm). Like adults.

LENGTH: 36-42 inches (91-107 cm).

Stuart's Milk Snake
Lampropeltis triangulum stuarti Williams, 1978

Stuart's Milk Snake has a black snout with a narrow white band forming a V. The rest of the head is black. The first black ring starts at the posterior edge of the parietals or one or two scale lengths posteriorly. The red scales lack black pigment or are moderately tipped with black.

LAMPROPELTIS TRIANGULUM STUARTI,
Stuart's Milk Snake

Stuart's Milk Snake combines a yellow snout band with relatively wide red rings and whitish rings that are heavily tipped with black. Many specimens probably would not be identifiable by the amateur. Photo by R. McCarthy.

The white scales have a moderate amount of black tipping. Red body rings number 19 to 28. This Milk Snake lives in dry tropical forests and the coastal plain. Adults reach 46 inches (117 cm) in length.

RANGE: Pacific slope of El Salvador, Honduras, Nicaragua, and northwestern Costa Rica.

MERISTICS: Dorsal scale rows 21; ventrals 219-242; subcaudals 49-59; supralabials 7-8; infralabials 8-11; red dorsal rings 19-28.

HEAD PATTERN: Snout black with a narrow white V; rest of head black.

DORSAL PATTERN: Red body rings 19-28, with very little or no black tipping. White scales moderately black-tipped. Red rings not as wide as black-white-black ring combination. The black rings appear widest, splitting the red rings middorsally.

VENTRAL PATTERN: All rings cross the belly. The white rings have some black patches, the black have some white, and the red rings have very little black.

JUVENILES: 8-9 inches (20-23 cm). Pattern like adults.

LENGTH: 40-46 inches (102-117 cm).

Although generally resembling the Honduran Milk Snake (and sometimes sold as that subspecies), the black scale tipping in the whitish rings and the generally paler colors are distinctive of *stuarti*. Photo by Guido Dingerkus.

L. t. syspila. Photo by R. G. Markel.

Red Milk Snake
Lampropeltis triangulum syspila (Cope, 1888)

The Red Milk Snake has a black band on the posterior part of the parietals or the parietals are nearly covered with black pigment; the rest of the head is red (or cream) with scattered black flecks. Red dorsal saddles are separated by black ventral borders from the first scale row on each side. Red body saddles number 16 to 31. Very variable in details of pattern and color because of extensive intergradation. Woods and rocky, grass-covered hillsides are the typical habitats. Adults reach 40 inches (102 cm).

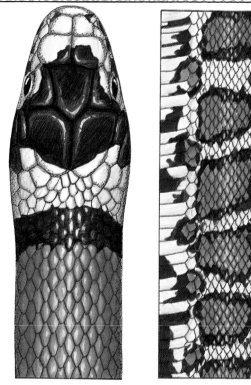

The Red Milk Snake often looks like an Eastern Milk Snake with a distinctive head pattern. Note the spots on the lower sides. Photo by Ken Lucas, Steinhart Aquarium.

LAMPROPELTIS TRIANGULUM SYSPILA, Red Milk Snake

RANGE: Southern Indiana and western Kentucky to southeastern Dakotas and eastern Oklahoma. At the eastern edge of the range it intergrades broadly with *L. t. triangulum* and the two become almost impossible to separate. Also intergrades broadly with *L. t. gentilis* and *anmaura*.

In the western and southern parts of the range, *L. t. syspila* is often distinctly tricolored. Photo by R. G. Markel.

MERISTICS: Dorsal scale rows 21; ventrals 170-212; subcaudals 37-51; supralabials 7; infralabials 8-10; red dorsal rings 16-31.

HEAD PATTERN: Snout red, sometimes with a thin black band; rest of head red, with a black-bordered white spot above each eye. Red sometimes replaced in whole or part by cream or tan.

DORSAL PATTERN: Red body rings (actually saddles) 16-31. Saddles do not extend ventrally below scale row one and are bordered ventrally by black rings. White bands expand ventrolaterally. Traces of a second row of small, dark ventrolateral blotches often present , weakest anteriorly.

VENTRAL PATTERN: Checkered with black and white, red absent.

JUVENILES: 8-9 inches (20-23 cm). Pattern similar to adults.

LENGTH: 21-28 inches (53-71 cm).

The Utah Milk Snake closely resembles *L. t. celaenops* but has an even more reduced pattern.
Photo by R. G. Markel.

Utah Milk Snake
Lampropeltis triangulum taylori Tanner and Loomis, 1957

The Utah Milk Snake often has an entirely black snout. The red rings are separated by black from the first scale row or edge of the ventrals. Black pigment frequently splits the red rings middorsally. The red body rings number 23 to 34. Habitats include ponderosa pine and Gambel oak with Rocky Mountain juniper and skunkbush. Adults reach 30 inches (76 cm).

RANGE: Central and northeastern Utah, western Colorado, and northern Arizona.

MERISTICS: Dorsal scale rows 21; ventrals 174-197; subcaudals 37-52; supralabials 7; infralabials 7-11; red dorsal rings 23-34.

The Utah Milk Snake is seldom available commercially. Photo by D. Breidenbach.

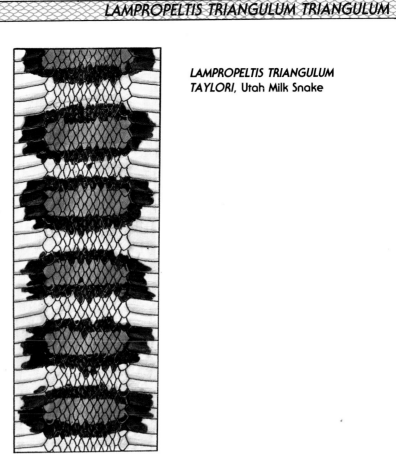

LAMPROPELTIS TRIANGULUM TAYLORI, Utah Milk Snake

HEAD PATTERN: Snout black or with pale mottling. Head more white than black, black on top.

DORSAL PATTERN: Red body rings range from 23 to 34. Black rings frequently encroaching on red and splitting red rings middorsally. First white ring encroaches on black at side of head. White rings as wide as the red rings and extending onto belly.

VENTRAL PATTERN: Mostly pale, with some black pigment from the black rings bordering the red rings above the ventrals.

JUVENILES: 7-8 inches (18-20 cm). Like adults.

LENGTH: 24-30 inches (61-76 cm).

Eastern Milk Snake
Lampropeltis triangulum triangulum (Lacepede, 1788)

The Eastern Milk Snake has the first dorsal blotch (not a ring in this subspecies) extending onto the head to form a Y or V. The body pattern consists of a row of dorsal saddles that

The typical Eastern Milk Snake has a *mexicana*-like forked nuchal blotch and lacks the tricolored pattern. Photo by R. G. Markel.

111

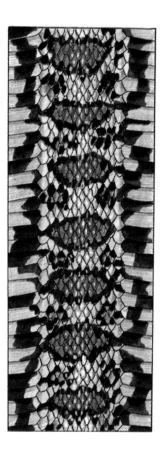

LAMPROPELTIS TRIANGULUM TRIANGULUM, Eastern Milk Snake

usually extend to the third or fourth scale row on each side and a ventrolateral row of small, irregularly 'shaped blotches. The saddles usually are reddish brown or gray with black borders. The major dorsal saddles number 26 to 54. Habitats include prairies, fields, woods, bogs, lake and ocean beaches, and stream edges. This subspecies shows a preference for rocky, forested hillsides. For a discussion of the sympatric association and intergradation with *L. t. elapsoides*, see the latter subspecies. Adults reach 5 feet (152 cm).

RANGE: Maine to Minnesota, south to northern Alabama, Tennessee, Georgia, and North Carolina, west to Illinois and Kentucky. In Canada it occurs from the northern edge of Georgian Bay and east of Lake Huron, including southern Quebec. Intergrades to the southeast with *L. t. elapsoides* and to the west with *L. t. syspila*.

MERISTICS: Dorsal scale rows 21; ventrals 182-214; subcaudals 35-54; supralabials 7-8; infralabials 7-11; dorsal saddles 26-54.

HEAD PATTERN: Snout light, with very thin dark lines between the scales; first dorsal saddle has arms extending onto the head to form a V or Y (occasionally absent).

This juvenile *L. t. triangulum* clearly shows the lateral spotting of the subspecies. The red color may be retained by adults. Photo by J. Dommers.

DORSAL PATTERN: Three to five black-bordered reddish brown saddles and blotches across the body, the smaller lateral blotches alternating with the larger middorsal saddles. Ground color tan or grayish, sometimes brighter. Middorsal saddles average 37.

VENTRAL PATTERN: Checkered with black on white, often irregular.

JUVENILES: 8-9 inches (20-23 cm). The blotches in young specimens are brighter red and contrast more with the black borders and white or ashen background.

LENGTH: 36-45 inches (91-114 cm).

Mountain Kingsnake
Lampropeltis zonata (Lockington, 1876)

The Mountain Kingsnake or California Mountain Kingsnake has a dorsal pattern of black and white rings with the white rings numbering more than 30. Often the black rings are split into two by red, producing the typical black-red-black-white-black pattern of the tricolored kingsnakes. The term triad is used for

When trying to identify Mountain Kingsnake subspecies, remember that counting triads—any black ring (split by red or not) and its bordering white rings—is important. The subspecies are all very similar. Photo by B. Kahl.

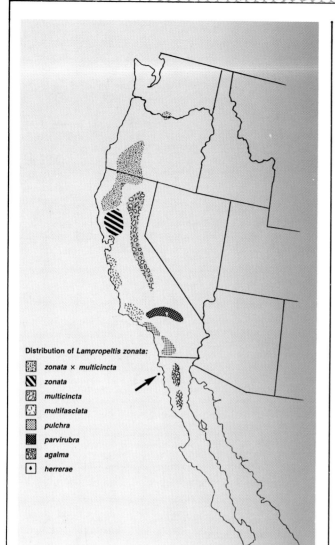

Distribution of *Lampropeltis zonata*:

- zonata × multicincta
- zonata
- multicincta
- multifasciata
- pulchra
- parvirubra
- agalma
- herrerae

Oregon and southward in the eastern part of the Coastal Ranges (avoiding the moist coastal regions) to the area north of San Francisco Bay. The rest of the range is comprised of disjunct populations, with a northern population in south-central Washington and isolated populations south of San Francisco Bay into northern Baja California. The species occurs from sea level (on South Todos Santos Island) to elevations of 8000 feet (2400 m) in the San Gabriel Mountains of Los Angeles County, California. Food taken includes lizards, rodents, and birds. Goodman and Goodman (1976) suggested that the tricolor pattern of *L. zonata* may be used in enticement displays. Snakes of this species were observed to lie in the open and elicit attacks from nesting birds. The snake would then use the frequency of attacks and the bird's behavior to locate the nest containing young birds. They described this phenomenon in *L. z. parvirubra* in the San Bernardino Mountains. Little appears to be known of the details of the natural history of this species. REVISIONS: Zweifel, 1952; Zweifel, 1974.

San Pedro Mountain Kingsnake
Lampropeltis zonata agalma Van Denburgh and Slevin, 1923

The San Pedro Mountain Kingsnake is a small snake that has more than half its pairs of black rings enclosing a red ring. The posterior edge of the first white ring crosses the last upper labials.

Most of the black rings of *L. z. agalma* are heavily split with red. Photo by V. N. Scheidt.

any black ring and its bordering white rings, whether or not the black includes red blotches or even complete rings. Thus the pattern white-black-white-black-red-black-white is two triads when rings are being counted. The white rings do not widen as they approach the belly, as they tend to do in *L. triangulum* and *L. getulus*. The snout may be black or black speckled with red, but not white. Supralabials usually are 7, infralabials 9. The last two maxillary teeth are usually longer and stouter than the ones in front. According to Zweifel (1974), the main portion of the range extends from northern Kern County, California, northward along the western flanks of the Sierra Nevadas into southwestern

LAMPROPELTIS ZONATA AGALMA, San Pedro Mountain Kingsnake

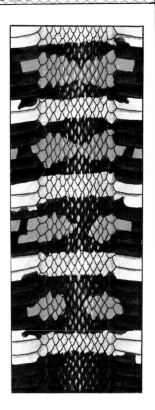

There are more than 40 triads, with a considerable amount of red present. There is much red on the snout. Adults reach 30 inches (76 cm).

RANGE: Northern Baja California, Sierra Juarez and Sierra San Pedro Martir.

MERISTICS: Dorsal scale rows 21-23; ventrals 194-220; subcaudals 50-56; body triads 41-48.

DORSAL PATTERN: Snout with red often heavy. Body with more than 40 triads, displaying a considerable amount of red, more than half the triads containing red rings.

VENTRAL PATTERN: Red encircles the belly along with intermittent black rings and continuations of the white rings.

JUVENILES: 7 inches (18 cm).

LENGTH: 24-30 inches (61-76 cm).

Todos Santos Island Kingsnake
Lampropeltis zonata herrerae Van Denburgh and Slevin, 1923

The Todos Santos Island Kingsnake lacks red in the triads, so its pattern may resemble that of the California Kingsnake, *L. getulus californiae*. The posterior edge of the first white ring is before the angle of the mouth. Adults reach 30 inches (76 cm). The natural history of this restricted form is virtually unknown and specimens are almost unavailable.

RANGE: Restricted to South Todos Santos Island, northern Baja California, about 50 miles (80 km) south of the California line.

MERISTICS: Dorsal scale rows 23; ventrals 216-220; subcaudals 53-59; body triads 36-41.

DORSAL PATTERN: Snout black. 36-41 triads on the body, virtually without red pigment in the black rings. Wide black rings alternate with narrower white rings. There may be faint traces of red on the lower scale rows.

VENTRAL PATTERN: Black and white rings with minute amounts of red.

JUVENILES: 7-8 inches (18-20 cm).

LENGTH: 24-30 inches (61-76 cm).

LAMPROPELTIS ZONATA HERRERAE, Todos Santos Island Kingsnake

Sierra Mountain Kingsnake
Lampropeltis zonata multicincta (Yarrow, 1882)

The Sierra Mountain Kingsnake has fewer than 60% of its body triads with the red confluent middorsally and thus forming complete rings. The posterior margin of the first white ring is behind the mouth. Wooded areas and shaded areas of canyons are its habitats. This is a rather small, slender, tricolored kingsnake with a relatively large range. Adults reach 40 inches (102 cm).

RANGE: Sierra Nevadas from Kern County and Tulare County to Shasta County, California. Intergrades with the St. Helena Mountain Kingsnake occur north into southwestern Oregon (beyond the present range of both parent subspecies).

MERISTICS: Dorsal scale rows 23; ventrals 202-227; subcaudals 46-61; body triads 23-48.

DORSAL PATTERN: Head and snout mostly black. 23 to 48 body triads, averaging 35; fewer than 60% of the triads contain red blotches confluent middorsally into a complete ring. Occasionally red may be absent, especially in the Yosemite National Park area.

L. z. multicincta shares a black snout with *parvirubra, pulchra,* and *zonata,* as well as *herrerae.* Photo by S. McKeown.

In some areas *multicincta* completely lacks red splitting the black, as in *herrerae,* but the first white ring ends behind the mouth. Photo by R. G. Markel.

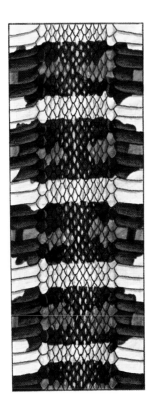

LAMPROPELTIS ZONATA MULTICINCTA,
Sierra Mountain Kingsnake

VENTRAL PATTERN: Black crosses the belly and allows some red to enter the ventral pattern. White rings cross the ventrals but are sometimes broken. May have a pattern of black, white, and red alternating areas.

JUVENILES: 7 inches (18 cm). Hatchlings have little red.

LENGTH: 30-36 inches (76-91 cm).

Coastal Mountain Kingsnake
Lampropeltis zonata multifasciata (Bocourt, 1886)

The Coastal Mountain Kingsnake has more red on the snout than the other subspecies. The black rings usually are narrow, especially on the sides. There are fewer than 41 body triads, but they contain large amounts of red. The posterior edge of the first white ring is over the last upper labial (southern populations) or over the angle of the mouth (northern populations). Wooded areas and shaded canyons are typical habitats. Adults reach about 36 inches (91 cm).

RANGE: Area south of San Francisco south to the Santa Clara River, Ventura County, California. Mostly coastal.

MERISTICS: Dorsal scale rows 23; ventrals 205-224; subcaudals 52-62; body triads 26-41.

DORSAL PATTERN: Snout with much red speckling. 26-41 body triads, averaging 35. More than 60% of the black rings are completely split by red

In *L. z. multifasciata* the red in most triads is in the form of a broad band, producing a pattern very similar to that of a milk snake. Photo by S. McKeown.

Evenly ringed specimens of the Coastal Mountain Kingsnake, *L. z. multifasciata*, differ from *L. triangulum* by having well over 30 red rings (usually many fewer in *triangulum*) and having the black rings narrowed at the lower scale row. Photo by B. E. Baur.

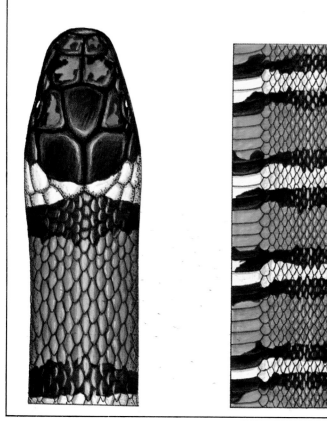

LAMPROPELTIS ZONATA MULTIFASCIATA,
Coastal Mountain Kingsnake

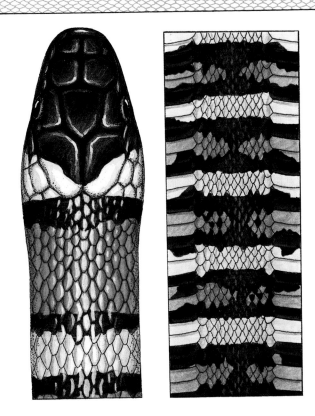

LAMPROPELTIS ZONATA PARVIRUBRA, San Bernardino Mountain Kingsnake

L. z. parvirubra looks much like *L. z. pulchra* but has more triads and only about one-third of the triads completely split by red (70% in *pulchra*). These are only average characters, however, and single specimens are best determined based on locality. Photo above by R. G. Markel, that below by B. E. Baur.

confluent middorsally. The black bands usually are narrow, especially low on the sides. The snake gives the appearance of having a great deal of red, especially in the Santa Cruz Mountains.

VENTRAL PATTERN: Red, black, and white rings encircle the body. Black pigment is scattered in the red rings.

JUVENILES: 7 inches (18 cm). Hatchlings have wide red rings bordered by thin black rings; the white rings are wider than the black and uniform in width.

LENGTH: 30-36 inches (76-91 cm).

San Bernardino Mountain Kingsnake
Lampropeltis zonata parvirubra Zweifel, 1952

The San Bernardino Mountain Kingsnake has at least 35 triads (usually 37 or more). The snout is dark, and the posterior margin of the first white ring is at least on or anterior to the last upper labial. This subspecies feeds on newborn rodents, small snakes, and lizards. Its habitats include foothills, canyons, and wooded areas of southern California. Adults reach 40 inches (102 cm).

RANGE: Los Angeles, San Bernardino, and central Riverside Counties, southern California.

MERISTICS: Dorsal scale rows 21; ventrals 204-220; subcaudals 48-60; body triads 35-48.

DORSAL PATTERN: Snout and head black. 35-48 body triads, average about 41. Usually fewer than 60% of the black rings are split by red bands confluent middorsally (actual average about one-third). White rings narrow. Black rings narrow on sides but usually (two-thirds) confluent middorsally, restricting the red to lateral blotches. The yellowish white ring scales may be tipped with black, giving a muddy appearance.

VENTRAL PATTERN: Red and white bands crossing onto the belly; little black present.

JUVENILES: 7-8 inches (18-20 cm). Light rings may appear whiter than in adults.

LENGTH: 36-40 inches (91-102 cm).

San Diego Mountain Kingsnake
Lampropeltis zonata pulchra Zweifel, 1952

The San Diego Mountain Kingsnake has the first white ring on or anterior to the last upper

LAMPROPELTIS ZONATA PULCHRA, San Diego Mountain Kingsnake

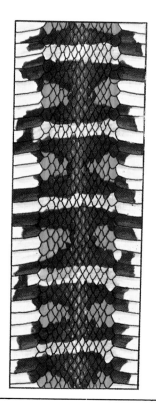

A San Diego Mountain Kingsnake with most of the triads completely split by wide red rings. Photo by R. S. Funk.

labial, as in the San Bernardino Mountain subspecies. However, there are 38 or fewer triads on the body. Adults to about 36 inches (91 cm).

RANGE: Los Angeles, Orange, Riverside, and San Diego Counties, southern California.

MERISTICS: Dorsal scale rows 21-23; ventrals 194-220; subcaudals 47-59; body triads 27-38.

DORSAL PATTERN: No red on snout. Fewer than 38 body triads, usually about 32. About 70% of the triads have the black rings split by red blotches confluent middorsally into full rings.

Less typical of *pulchra* is this specimen with few red bands complete across the middorsal area, the black of the triads not completely split. Photo by R. S. Funk.

Because of the bright colors and the extensive amount of red, *L. zonata pulchra* is probably the most popular subspecies of Mountain Kingsnake. Photo by Ken Lucas, Steinhart Aquarium.

VENTRAL PATTERN: Black rings narrow as they enter the venter, allowing much red to appear in the belly pattern.
JUVENILES: 7 inches (18 cm). Like adults.
LENGTH: 30-36 inches (76-91 cm).

St. Helena Mountain Kingsnake
Lampropeltis zonata zonata (Lockington, 1876)
The St. Helena Mountain Kingsnake has the posterior margin of the first white ring behind the posterior angle of the mouth. Red blotches split the black rings and are confluent middorsally in more than 60% of the triads. The snout is black or dark. This poorly known subspecies feeds upon small snakes, lizards, and newborn rodents. Wooded areas are its habitat. Adults reach 40 inches (102 cm).
RANGE: Mendocino, Napa, and Sonoma Counties, California. Intergrades with the Sierra Mountain Kingsnake occur northward into southeastern Oregon; the Washington population also appears to be comprised of intergrades.
MERISTICS: Dorsal scale rows 23; ventrals 207-218; subcaudals 46-52; body triads 24-30.

LAMPROPELTIS ZONATA ZONATA, St. Helena Mountain Kingsnake

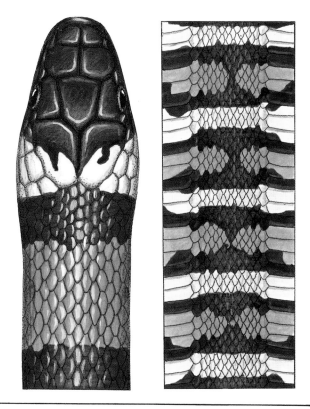

The poorly known St. Helena Mountain Kingsnake. Photo by Mike Dee.

DORSAL PATTERN: Snout dark, without red. Body triads 24 to 30, averaging 27 (limited material available to Zweifel). 60% of the triads are split by red confluent middorsally into complete rings, but occasionally the red may be absent. Red rings about as wide as black-white-black ring combination. White and black rings about equally wide, may be connected middorsally.
VENTRAL PATTERN: Red and white rings encircle the body; red rings with some black pigment.
JUVENILES: 7-8 inches (18-20 cm). White rings may be brighter than in adults.
LENGTH: 30-36 inches (76-91 cm).

The subspecies of *Lampropeltis zonata* often are not identifiable from single specimens without locality data. All the taxa are extremely similar and all are very variable.

Diseases and parasites

Research into the diseases and parasites of kingsnakes is still meager, but enough is known to mention some of the most common conditions seen in captive and wild-caught snakes. Also given here is information on the various drugs that have been used with varying success in treating these conditions. See Frye, 1973, and Ross, 1984, for more detailed information on many conditions and their treatment. It is best to simply try to keep your snakes in the best environments possible and avoid disease situations whenever possible. Stress is an enabling factor in many diseases. It is always best to work in conjunction with a knowledgeable veterinarian when attempting anything more than basic first aid.

Bacteria

The most commonly found bacteria in snakes belong to the genera *Pseudomonas, Aeromonas, Proteus, Klebsiella,* and *Citrobacter,* although a variety of other genera have been found on occasion, including staphylococci, *Moraxella, Serratia, Herellea, Mima,* and *Escherichia.*

Infectious stomatitis Infectious stomatitis (also known as mouth rot, ulcerative gingivitis, and ulcerative stomatitis) is the most common disease of captive snakes. The earliest sign is the production of unusual oral mucus. Some authors have suggested that a vitamin deficiency, especially of ascorbic acid (vitamin C), is a significant factor in the development of mouth rot. Diagnosis is based on finding lesions in the mouth. The following antibiotics possess, in decreasing order, the greatest practical antibacterial activity: gentamicin, chloramphenicol, kanamycin, neomycin, cephalothin, streptomycin, ampicillin, and tetracycline. This list is not meant to supplant culturing and sensitivity tests, but is included as an aid in selecting a drug while waiting for the results of specific tests.

The proper diet can be supplemented with 10 to 50 mg ascorbic acid, but use force-feeding only as a last resort. Improvement of the

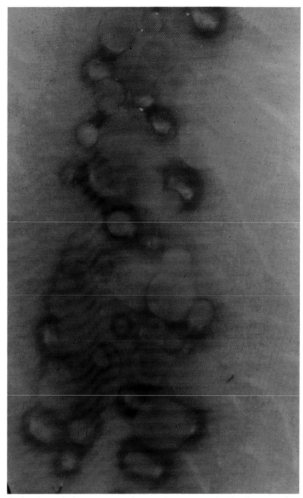

Colonies of *Aeromonas* bacteria are typical of several diseases of snakes.

environment, especially the humidity and temperature, is important since normal host defense mechanisms such as tissue repair and antibody production are temperature-dependent. Ulceration and caseation (cheesy tissue build-up) should be cleansed with cotton swabs soaked in hydrogen peroxide or betadine solution. Water for soaking, drinking, or swimming should be treated routinely with triple sulfa solution (Tri-sulfa-G, Norden) at 1 oz/gal.

Abscesses Abscesses usually are firm swellings that may occur on any part of the body. Treatment involves incision and curettage with subsequent applications of Lugol's solution. An antibiotic ointment containing proteolytic enzymes should be applied until healing is certain.

Traumatic lesions

The most traumatic lesion encountered in captive snakes is rat bites. Rat bites can be serious, but normally debridement and application of Furacin are the only treatments required. The problem of rat bites can be avoided by not feeding conscious, living rats to snakes. Simply stunning the rats usually will eliminate the hazard of bite trauma.

Another frequently seen traumatic lesion is abrasion of the rostral scale. Abraded areas should be gently cleansed and treated topically with an appropriate ointment such as nitrofurazone (Furacin, Eaton).

Burns

The use of unprotected overhead heat lamps is usually the cause of burns in captive snakes. A useful alternative to heat lamps is the employment of heating coils or thermal pads beneath the cage. Dress burns with Furacin ointment until healed.

Shedding problems

Impaired skin shedding (dysecdysis) is a common problem in captive snakes. In the normal course of events, a snake will refuse food for seven to ten days before shedding. The eyes become progressively duller and eventually appear to be opaque. This opacity fades just before the shed. At the same time, the skin coloration becomes dull. These changes result from oil secretion between the old and underlying healthy epidermis layers. If a snake is dehydrated or otherwise debilitated, the process of shedding may be impaired or delayed. Soaking the snake in tepid water aids in the gentle removal of dried, non-separated skin. An adequate water supply and cage decorations such as logs and branches are essential for easy shedding. Occasionally a snake will fail to shed

Shedding difficulties are a common problem in all snakes. If the snake is healthy and the humidity is correct, the problem usually resolves itself, but the keeper may have to carefully remove old skin from around the head. Photo by S. Kochetov.

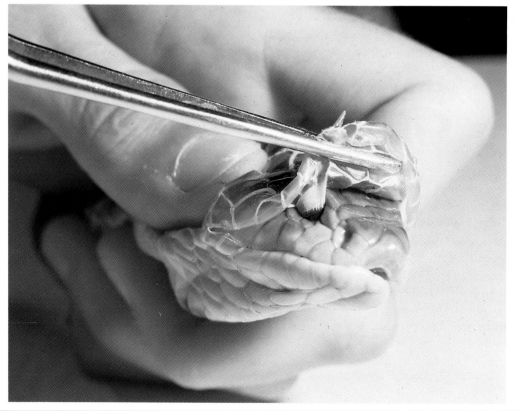

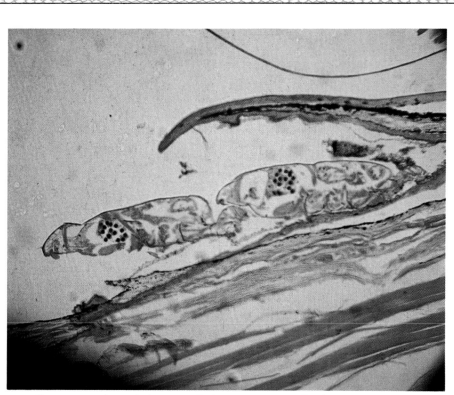

Cross-section through the mite *Ophionyssus natricus* feeding under a scale. Photo by Dr. E. Elkan.

one or both of the corneal shields, causing temporary blindness. The shields can be removed easily by gentle lifting with a pair of fine forceps. If the shields do not part with relative ease, the application of warm, moist compresses will further aid in their removal.

Ophthalmic diseases

Probably the most frequently encountered eye problem in captive kingsnakes is panophthalmitis with orbital abscessation. Upon inspection the eye appears to be completely obliterated. Incision and drainage from beneath the orbital tissues may result in return to full function. A small incision, either via the oral cavity or immediately beneath the corneal shield, will provide access to the site of the retrocorneal shield. Thickened pus and cellular detritus can be removed gently with a smooth probe or flattened curette. Flushing with Ringer's solution to which neomycin sulfate solution has been added aids in removing any residual debris. Parenteral antibiotic coverage should also be provided. Needless to say, all this is a job for a qualified veterinarian.

Parasites

Ectoparasites Snakes quite frequently carry ectoparasites such as mites (especially *Ophionyssus natricus*) and ticks (especially *Ornithodoros*). The simplest way of eliminating mites and ticks is to suspend small pieces of a dichlorvos-impregnated plastic pest strip above the cage for a few days. Soaking individual specimens in tepid water has also proved successful.

Myiasis with the larvae of *Cuterebra*, *Calitroga*, *Sarcophaga*, and other screwflies and fleshflies is also seen. Removal of the larvae, debridement, and local wound treatment are usually sufficient to bring about healing.

Ameba *Endamoeba invadens* is the causative agent in snake ulcerative gastritis, enteritis, and hepatitis. The stomach, large and small

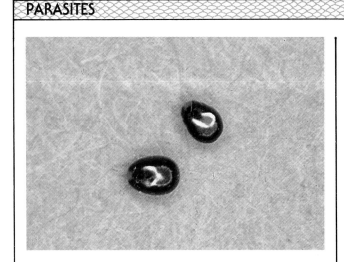

intestine, and liver are most frequently involved in amebiasis. The parasites spread within the host via the blood and lymph vessels. Ulcers and necrosis are commonly observed. Massive hepatic necrosis may occur if the hepatic portal venous branches are obstructed by thromboemboli. Renal necrosis also has been reported to be caused by *E. invadens*. Intramuscular injections of emetine hydrochloride (E. Lilly) at a dosage of 0.5 mg/kg may be given daily for ten days. Hydration of the patient must be maintained at all times to prevent excessive serum levels due to hemoconcentration.

Flagellates Hemoflagellates, especially *Trypanosoma butananense, T. erythrolampi, T. mattogrossense,* and *T. merremi,* have been found in some South American snakes. An unclassified trypanosome from a ventral cervical cyst in a California kingsnake (*Lampropeltis getulus californiae*) has been found; microfilariae were also found. All attempts at more definitive identification of these parasites have failed. Other hemoflagellates that reportedly have been found in clinically healthy snakes are

Ticks are among the parasites most likely to be noticed on wild-caught kingsnakes. Most often they look like small dark grains (above). The heavily barbed mouthparts of *Ornithodoros* are visible in the cross-section below. Photo above by M. Gilroy, that below by Dr. E. Elkan.

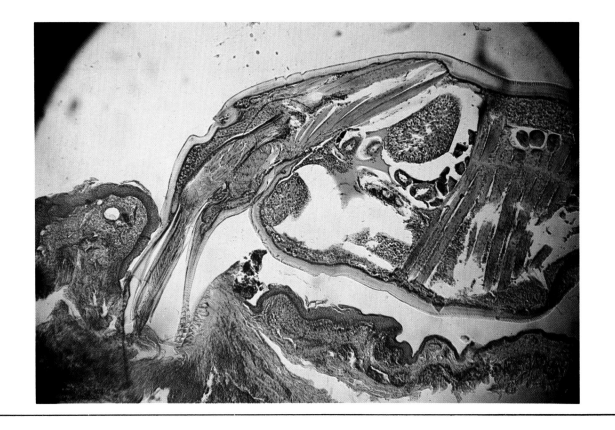

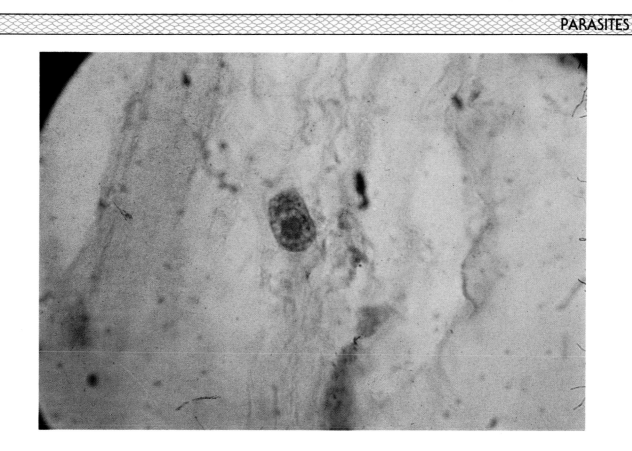

The parasitic ameba *Endamoeba invadens* is a serious threat to snakes as it may cause extensive internal damage to several organs. The treatment with emetine hydrochloride is also debilitating to the snake. Photos by Dr. E. Elkan.

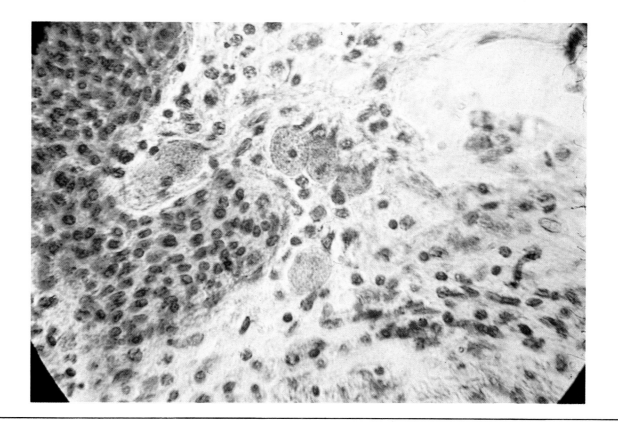

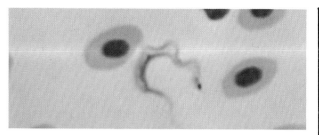

Trypanosoma is a flagellate commonly found in the blood of snakes.

Herpetomonas homalosoma var., *Eutrichomastix serpentis, Chilomastix* sp., *Trichomonas* sp., and *Giardia* sp.

Sporozoans Coccidial infections of the gall bladder with *Eimeria bitis* have been reported. *Isospora naiae* has also been reported to produce gall bladder and intestinal pathology. Sulfamethazine or sulfadimethoxine at the appropriate dosage should be instituted as soon as positive diagnosis is made from stool samples. Sporozoan parasites of the genus *Haemogregarina* are frequently seen in snake blood. There are many species within this genus. As yet, *Haemogregarina* has not been proved to be implicated in clinical disease in snakes.

Worms Nematodes, cestodes, and trematodes have been found in reptiles. Since the diet of most snakes consists of living animals of many different species that serve as intermediate hosts for these parasites, exposure of the snakes is assured.

The tongueworms *Armillifer grandis* (large) and *armillatus* (small). Photo by R.-Klinke.

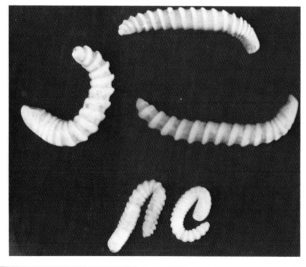

A number of tongueworms or linguatulids, enigmatic worm-like parasites that are probably related to the arthropods, pass through the egg and larval stages in one host and through nymphal and adult stages in another. Most commonly a fish or mammal is the intermediate host, and the most common genus is probably *Armillifer*. After completing a migration through the body during development from the larval stage, the mature *Armillifer* destroy pulmonary tissue. Cysts are passed via the sputum of the infected snake. To avoid cross-contamination by water bowls, cages, hands, etc., careful attention must be given to hygiene. No effective treatment is known. Recognized carriers should be either isolated or destroyed.

There are myriads of both cestode (tapeworms) and nematode (roundworms) parasites that infest kingsnakes. Niclosamide (Yomesan, Chemagro) is effective against cestodes when the dosage is tailored to the body weight and physical condition of the patient. Both piperazine citrate and thiabendazole have been used successfully for nematode parasites. Use carefully and dose correctly. Vermifuges are most easily administered via stomach tube. Examination of stool samples will usually allow identification of the tapes and roundworms present.

A number of species of flukes (trematodes) are found in almost all captive snakes that are wild-bred. Some are easily seen on physical examinations of the pharynx or eyes. The flukes most commonly seen in reptiles belong to the family Ochetosomatidae. These are often found in the respiratory and upper digestive tracts of snakes.

Pseudoneoplasms

Pseudoneoplasms are firm to fluctuant swellings most frequently found in terrestrial snakes. In every case, helminth parasites, hemogregarines, and trypanosomes were found in mixed infections. Histopathologically, these lesions represent eosinophilic granulomata and verminous cysts. Treatment consists of thorough excision, debridement, and packing with an appropriate medication such as providone-impregnated gauze sponges, mild silver nitrate, or 4% buffered formalin.

Medications Used in Captive Snakes

Generic/Trade Names	Route	Frequency	Dosage	Indications
Amikacin (Amikin)	Subcutaneous (SC)	Every (Q) 72 hrs for 5 injections	1.25 mg. /lb	1,5,6,12,2
Carbenicillin (Geopen)	SC	Daily for 6 days	25–50 mg. /lb	11,4
Chloramphenicol (Chlormycetin)	SC	Q 12 hrs for 6 days	5–15 mg. /lb per inj.	2,3,11
Gentamycin (Gentocin)	SC	Q 72 hrs for 5 injections	1.25 mg. /lb	7,1,3,8,11
Netilmicin (Netromycin)	SC	Q 72 hrs for 5 injections	1.25 mg. /lb	4,12,9,2,3
Trimethoprim-Sulfa (Di-Trim)	SC	Daily for 5 days	1 cc /lb	10,5,11,1,7
Tobramycin (Nebcin)	SC	Q 72 hrs for 5 injections	1.25 mg. /lb	9,11,5,6,7
Tylosin (Tylan)	SC	Daily for 6 days	20–30 mg. /lb	7th choice for 4
Metronidazole (Flagyl)	Orally	Once, repeat in 14 days	40 mg. /lb	A,B,C,D,E,F
Emetine Hcl	SC	Daily for 10 days	6 mg. /lb	G
Levamisole (Levasole)	SC	2 injections, 10 days apart	0.2 cc /lb Diluted	H
Praziquantel (Droncit)	SC	Once, may repeat in 14 days	0.1 cc /350 grams	I
Ketoconazol (Nizoral)	SC	Q 12 hrs for 6 days	1.25 mg. /lb	J
Nystatin (1000 units)	Orally	Daily for 6 days	0.6 cc /lb	J
Vit. B Complex	SC	Daily as needed	0.06 cc /lb	K
Dichlorvos (No-Pest Strip)	Suspended above cage	24 hours	1 Strip/1000 cu ft room space	L

Medications Used in Captive Snakes

Generic/Trade Names	Route	Frequency	Dosage	Indications
Allopurinal (Zyloprim)	Orally	Daily for 7–10 days	100 mg. /lb	M
Sulfamethazine (AS 250)	SC	Daily for 6 days	5 mg. /lb	N
Chloroquine (Aralen)	SC	Every other day times 3	1.25 mg. /lb	N
Chloroquine (Aralen)	SC	Every other day times 3	0.6 mg. /lb	O
Dexamethasone (Azium)	SC	Daily for 1–5 days, max. 5 in 30 days	0.08–0.5 mg. /lb	P
Ketamine HCL (Vetalar)	SC	Single injection	5–10 mg. /lb	Q
Piperazine Citrate (Pipersol)	Orally	No more than every 14 days	25 mg. /lb	R
Tetrachlorethylene (Nema)	Orally	Once 4 days after fed, repeat 3–4 wks	0.25 cc /lb	G

Indications Index

1) *Acinetobacter*
2) *Aeromonas*
3) *Citrobacter*
4) *Enterobacter*
5) *Flavobacter*
6) *Klebisella*
7) *Providencia*
8) *Pseudomonas aeruginosa*
9) *Pseudomonas fluorescens*
10) *Pseudomonas malthopila*
11) *Pseudomonas* (other)
12) *Serritia*

A *Entamoeba invadens*
B *Trichomonas*
C *Balantidium*
D Rhizopoda
E Flagellates
F Ciliates
G Trematodes (flukes)
H Nematodes (roundworms)
I Tapeworms
J Yeast infections
K Debilitation
L Ectoparasites
M Uric acid
N Blood Protozoa
O Trypanosomes, hemogregarines & plasmodia
P Shock/stress inflammation
Q Anesthesia
R Metazoan parasites

Human Injectibles

Generic Name	Trade Name	Manufacturer
Amikacin	Amikin	Bristol
Trimethoprim-Sulfa	Bactrim, Septra	Roche, Burroughs, Wellcome
Cefoperozone	Cefobid	Roerig-Pfizer
Chloramphenicol	Chlormycetin	Parke Davis
Emetine Hcl	Emetine Hcl	Eli Lilly
Gentamycin	Garamycin	Schering
Netilmicin	Netromycin	Schering
Tobramycin	Nebcin	Eli Lilly
Ampicillin	Polycillin	Bristol

Veterinary Injectibles

Generic Name	Trade Name	Manufacturer
Dexamethasone	Azium	Schering
Vit. B Complex	B-Complex-Plus	Frank Vet Inc.
Trimethoprim-Sulfa	Di-Trim	Diamond
Praziquantel	Droncit	Ba Vet
Levamisole	Levasole	Pitman-Moore
Chloramphenicol	Mychel	Rachelle
Ketocanazol	Nizoral	Janssen
Ampicillin	Polyflex	Bristol
Tylosin	Tylan	Elanco
Ketamine	Vetalar	Parke Davis

Human and Veterinary Oral Drugs

Generic Name	Trade Name	Designation	Manufacturer
Chloroquine	Aralen	Human	Breon-Winthrop
Sulfamethazine	AS 250	Animal	Am. Cyanamid
Metronidazole	Flagyl	Human	Searle
Nystatin	Mycostatin	Human	Squibb
Tetrachlorethylene	Nema	Animal	Parke Davis
Piperazine Citrate	Pipersol	Animal	Burns-Biotec
Allopurinal	Zyloprim	Human	B.W.

Some Pattern and Scalation Details

Lampropeltis alterna, dorsal

Lampropeltis alterna, ventral

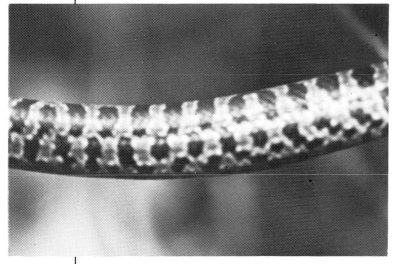

Lampropeltis c. calligaster, dorsal

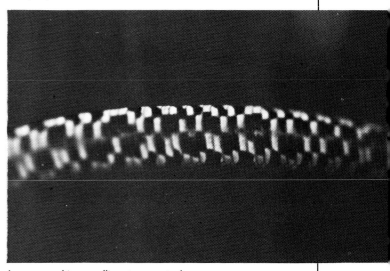

Lampropeltis c. calligaster, ventral

Lampropeltis g. californiae, albino, dorsal

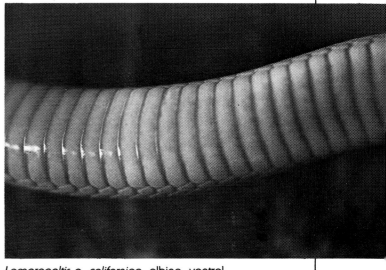

Lampropeltis g. californiae, albino, ventral

133

Lampropeltis g. californiae, ringed

Lampropeltis g. californiae, striped

Lampropeltis g. getulus, dorsal

Lampropletis g. getulus, ventral

Lampropeltis g. floridana, dorsal

Lampropeltis g. floridana, ventral

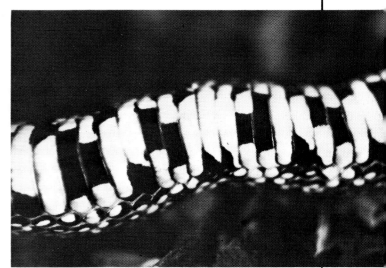

Lampropeltis g. holbrooki, dorsal

Lampropeltis g. holbrooki, ventral

Lampropeltis t. gentilis, dorsal

Lampropeltis t. gentilis, ventral

Lampropeltis t. sinaloae, dorsal

Lampropeltis t. sinaloae, ventral

All photos by R. G. Markel

Glossary

ABDOMEN: Lower surface of the body between the neck and the cloaca.

ANAL PLATE: Scale in front of cloaca. Single or divided; when divided, the seam is oblique.

BILOBED: Having two lobes.

BODY: In a snake, the section from nape to cloaca.

CLOACA: Posterior opening of both the excretory and reproductive tracts. In reptiles and amphibians solid wastes, semiliquid uric acids, and reproductive cells exit through the cloaca.

COLUBRID: Snakes belonging to the family Colubridae.

DENTICULATE: Having tooth-like projections or serrations.

DERMAL: Relating to the skin.

DORSAL: Pertaining to the back.

DORSAL SCALES: Scales on the dorsal surface of the body. Number of dorsal scale rows refers to counts around the middle of the body.

ECDYSIS: Shedding of the outer skin; molting.

FRONTAL: Median unpaired scale on top of the head between the eyes.

HEMIPENES: Paired evertible intromittent organs of the male snake and lizard.

INFRALABIALS: Enlarged scales lining the lower jaw.

INTERNASAL: Plates on top of the head (usually two) between the plates that surround or border the nostrils.

LABIALS: Enlarged scales bordering the mouth.

LOREAL: Scale on the side of the head between the nostril and the eye, but not touching either.

MANDIBLE: Lower jaw.

MAXILLA: Upper jaw.

MENTAL: Median scale at the tip of the lower jaw.

MIDDORSAL: Located on the median line of the back.

NASAL: Scale containing or bordering a nostril. Often a prenasal anterior to the nostril and a postnasal posterior to the nostril.

OCULAR: One of the scales forming the margin of the eye cavity. The supra-, pre-, post-, and suboculars are the scales respectively above, before, behind, and under the eye.

OVIPAROUS: Laying eggs.

PARIETALS: Pair of large scales on top of the head behind the frontal.

PREFRONTALS: Pair of large scales just before the frontal.

ROSTRAL: Median plate at front of snout bordering the anterior junction of the upper jaws.

SCALE ROWS: Number of rows of dorsal scales, counted obliquely. The number usually varies from one end of the body to the other, but the maximum number (usually at midbody) is meant. Scale rows in normal snakes are usually odd numbers; thus 21-23 scale rows means 21 or 23, not 21, 22, or 23.

SEX: In snakes, determined externally by the shape of the base of the tail, which is wide in males, narrow and more quickly tapering in females.

SHED: The cast off skin.

SUBCAUDALS: Enlarged scales under the tail.

SUPRALABIALS: Enlarged scales bordering the edge of the upper jaw.

TAIL: Part of a snake posterior to the cloaca.

TEMPORALS: More or less enlarged scales behind the postoculars and above the angle of the jaw.

VENTRALS: Enlarged strap-like scales covering the lower surface of the snake from the head to the anal scale.

Measurement Conversion Factors

When you know—	Multiply by—	To find—
Length:		
Millimeters (mm)	0.04	inches (in)
Centimeters (cm)	0.4	inches (in)
Meters (m)	3.3	feet (ft)
Meters (m)	1.1	yards (yd)
Kilometers (km)	0.6	miles (mi)
Inches (in)	2.54	centimeters (cm)
Feet (ft)	30	centimeters (cm)
Yards (yd)	0.9	meters (m)
Miles (mi)	1.6	kilometers (km)
Area:		
Square centimeters (cm^2)	0.16	square inches (sq in)
Square meters (m^2)	1.2	square yards (sq yd)
Square kilometers (km^2)	0.4	square miles (sq mi)
Hectares (ha)	2.5	acres
Square inches (sq in)	6.5	square centimeters (cm^2)
Square feet (sq ft)	0.09	square meters (m^2)
Square yards (sq yd)	0.8	square meters (m^2)
Square miles (sq mi)	1.2	square kilometers (km^2)
Acres	0.4	hectares (ha)
Mass (Weight):		
Grams (g)	0.035	ounces (oz)
Kilograms (kg)	2.2	pounds (lb)
Ounces (oz)	28	grams (g)
Pounds (lb)	0.45	kilograms (kg)
Volume:		
Milliliters (ml)	0.03	fluid ounces (fl oz)
Liters (L)	2.1	pints (pt)
Liters (L)	1.06	quarts (qt)
Liters (L)	0.26	U.S. gallons (gal)
Liters (L)	0.22	Imperial gallons (gal)
Cubic centimeters (cc)	16.387	cubic inches (cu in)
Cubic meters (cm^3)	35	cubic feet (cu ft)
Cubic meters (cm^3)	1.3	cubic yards (cu yd)
Teaspoons (tsp)	5	millimeters (ml)
Tablespoons (tbsp)	15	millimeters (ml)
Fluid ounces (fl oz)	30	millimeters (ml)
Cups (c)	0.24	liters (L)
Pints (pt)	0.47	liters (L)
Quarts (qt)	0.95	liters (L)
U.S. gallons (gal)	3.8	liters (L)
U.S. gallons (gal)	231	cubic inches (cu in)
Imperial gallons (gal)	4.5	liters (L)
Imperial gallons (gal)	277.42	cubic inches (cu in)
Cubic inches (cu in)	0.061	cubic centimeters (cc)
Cubic feet (cu ft)	0.028	cubic meters (m^3)
Cubic yards (cu yd)	0.76	cubic meters (m^3)
Temperature:		
Celsius (°C)	multiply by 1.8, add 32	Fahrenheit (°F)
Fahrenheit (°F)	subtract 32, multiply by 0.555	Celsius (°C)

References

Allen, W. B., Jr. 1986. *State Lists of Endangered and Threatened Species of Reptiles and Laws and Regulations Covering Collecting of Reptiles and Amphibians in Each State.* Privately published.

Alvarez, del Toro M. 1960. *Los Reptiles de Chiapas.* Instituto Zoologico Estado Tuxtla Gutierrez, Chiapas, Mexico.

Bechtel, H. B. 1978. "Color and pattern in snakes (Reptilia, Serpentes)," *J. Herpetology,* 12(4): 521–532.

Bechtel, H. B. and E. Bechtel. 1962. "Heredity of albinism in the corn snake, *Elaphe guttata guttata,* demonstrated in captive breeding," *Copeia,* 1962(2): 436-437.

Bechtel, H. B. and E. Bechtel. 1980. "Histochemical demonstration of two types of albinism in San Diego gopher snakes (*Pituophis melanoleucus annectens*) by use of dopa reaction," *Copeia,* 1980(4): 932–935.

Bechtel, H. B. and E. Bechtel. 1981. "Albinism in the snake *Elaphe obsoleta,*" *J. Herpetology,* 15(4): 397–402.

Blanchard, F. N. 1921. *Revision of the Kingsnakes, Genus* Lampropeltis. *Bull. 114, U. S. National Museum.* Washington, D.C.

Blaney, R. M. 1973. "*Lampropeltis.*" *Cat. Amer. Amphibians and Reptiles,* 150: 1-2.

Blaney, R. M. 1977. "Systematics of the common kingsnake, *Lampropeltis getulus* (Linnaeus)," *Tulane Stud. Zool. Bot.,* 19(3/4): 47-103.

Blaney, R. M. 1978. "*Lampropeltis calligaster.*" *Cat. Amer. Amphibians and Reptiles,* 229: 1-2.

Brattstrom, B. H. 1955. "Records of some Pliocene and Pleistocene reptiles and amphibians from Mexico," *Bull. S. Calif. Acad. Sci.,* 14(1): 1-4.

Cochran, D. and Goin, C. 1970. *The New Field Book of Reptiles and Amphibians.* G. P. Putnam and Sons, New York.

Collins, J. T., J. E. Huheey, J. L. Knight, and H. M. Smith. 1978. "Standard common and current scientific names for North American amphibians and reptiles," *SSAR Misc. Publ.,* 7: 36 pp.

Conant, R. 1958. *A Field Guide to the Reptiles and Amphibians.* Houghton Mifflin Co., Boston.

Conant, R. 1975. *A Field Guide to Reptiles and Amphibians of Eastern and Central North America.* Houghton Mifflin Co., Boston.

Ditmars, R. 1939. *Field Book of North American Snakes.* Doubleday and Co., New York.

Duellman, W. 1961. "The amphibians and reptiles of Michoacan, Mexico," *Misc. Publ. Univ. Kansas.*

Fitch, H. S. 1970. "Reproductive cycles in lizards and snakes," *Misc. Publ. Univ. Kansas,* 52.

Fowler, M. E. 1978. *Zoo and Wild Animal Medicine.* W. B. Saunders Co., Phila. Pa.

Frye, F. L. 1973. *Husbandry, Medicine and Surgery in Captive Reptiles.* VM Publishing, Bonner Springs, Kansas.

Garstka, W. R. 1982. "Systematics of the *mexicana* species group of the colubrid genus *Lampropeltis,* with an hypothesis mimicry," *Breviora (Mus. Comp. Zool.),* 466.

Gehlbach, F. and C. McCoy. 1965. "Additional observations on variation and distribution of the gray banded kingsnake, *Lampropeltis mexicana* (Garman)," *Herpetologica,* 21(1): 35-38.

Gehlbach, F. and J. Baker. 1962. "Kingsnakes allied with *Lampropeltis mexicana*: taxonomy and natural history," *Copeia,* 1962(2): 291-300.

Gehlbach, F. 1967. "*Lampropeltis mexicana.*" *Cat. Amer. Amphibians and Reptiles,* 55: 1-2.

Goodman, J. D. and J. M. Goodman. 1976. "Contrasting color and pattern enticement display in snakes," *Herpetologica*, 32(2): 148-150.

Guenther, A. C. 1893. *Biologia Centrali-Americana: Reptilia and Batrachia.* London.

Hamilton, W. J. and J. A. Pollack. 1955. "The food of some colubrid snakes from Fort Benning, Georgia," *Ecology*, 37: 519-526.

Hensley, M. 1959. "Albinism in North American amphibians and reptiles," *Publ. Mus. Michigan State Univ., Biol. Ser.*, 1(4):133–159.

Holman, J. A. 1964. "Fossil snakes from the Valentine Formation of Nebraska," *Copeia*, 1964(4): 631-637.

Klimstra, W. D. 1959. "Food habits of the yellow-bellied kingsnake in southern Illinois," *Herpetologica*, 15(1): 1-5.

Leviton, A. E. and B. H. Banta. 1964. "Midwinter reconnaissance of the herpetofauna of the Cape Region of Baja California, Mexico," *Proc. Calif. Acad. Sci.*, 30(7).

Lockwood, R. A. 1954. "Food habits of the mole snake," *Herpetologica*, 10(2): 110.

Nevers, P. and H. Saedler. 1977. "Transposable genetic elements as agents of gene instability and chromosomal rearrangements," *Nature*, 268: 109–114. 14 July.

Perkins, C. B. 1949. "The snakes of San Diego Co., with description and key," *Bull. Zool. Soc. San Diego*, 23.

Price, R. 1987. "Disjunct occurrence of mole snakes in peninsular Florida, and the description of a new subspecies of *Lampropeltis calligaster,*" *Bull. Chicago Herp. Soc.*, 22(9): 148.

Quinn, H. R. 1983. "Two new subspecies of *Lampropeltis triangulum* from Mexico," *Trans. Kansas Acad. Sci.*, 86(4): 113-135.

Ross, R. A. 1984. *The Bacterial Diseases of Reptiles.* Inst. Herp. Res., San Francisco, Calif.

Sanborn, S. R. and R. B. Loomis. 1976. *Keys to the Amphibians and Reptiles of Baja California, Mexico, and Adjacent Islands.* C. S. U. Long Beach.

Shaw, C. E. and S. Campbell. 1974. *Snakes of the American West.* Knopf, New York.

Smith, H. M. and E. Taylor. 1945. *An Annotated Check-list and Key to the Snakes of Mexico. Bull. 187, U. S. National Museum.* Washington, D. C.

Soule, M. and A. J. Sloan. 1966. "Biogeography and distribution of reptiles and amphibians of the islands in the Gulf of California, Mexico," *Trans. San Diego Soc. Nat. Hist.*, 14.

Stebbins, R. C. 1966. *A Field Guide to Western Reptiles and Amphibians.* Houghton Mifflin Co., Boston.

Tanner, W. W. 1953. "A study of the taxonomy and phylogeny of *Lampropeltis pyromelana* (Cope)," *Great Basin Naturalist*, 13(1/2): 47-66.

Tanzer, E. 1970. "Polymorphism in the *mexicana* complex of kingsnakes with notes on their natural history," *Herpetologica*, 26(4): 419-428.

Tryon, B.W. and J.B. Murphy. 1982. "Miscellaneous notes on the reproductive biology of reptiles. 5. Thirteen varieties of the genus *Lampropeltis*, species *mexicana*, *triangulum* and *zonata*," *Trans. Kansas Acad. Sci.*, 85: 96-119.

Webb, R. 1961. "A new kingsnake from Mexico, with remarks on the *mexicana* group of the genus *Lampropeltis*," *Copeia*, 1961(3): 326-333.

Williams, K. L. 1978. *Systematics and natural history of the American Milksnake,* Lampropeltis triangulum. *Milwaukee Pub. Mus. Publ., Biol. Geol.*, 2: 258 pp.

Witkop, C.J., Jr. 1975. "Albinism," *Natural History*, 84(8). October.

Wright, A. H. and A. A. Wright. 1957. *Handbook of Snakes of the United States and Canada.* Comstock, Ithaca.

Zweifel, R. G. 1952. "Pattern variations and evolution of the mountain kingsnake, *Lampropeltis zonata*," *Copeia*, 1952(3): 152-168.

Zweifel, R. G. 1974. "*Lampropeltis zonata.*" *Cat. Amer. Amphibians and Reptiles*, 174: 1-4.

Index

(**Bold** page numbers indicate illustrations)